RESTORING PEACE

USING LESSONS FROM PRISON TO MEND

BROKEN RELATIONSHIPS

Bridges To Life Program Edition

By

Kirk Blackard

Foreword by

John Sage, Founder and Executive Director, Bridges To Life

RESTORING PEACE

Using Lessons From Prison to Mend Broken Relationships

Bridges To Life Program Edition

ISBN: 0-9766989-1-9

BRIDGES TO LIFE BOOKS

PRINTED IN THE UNITED STATES OF AMERICA

For information or to order additional copies, contact:

Bridges To Life
P.O. Box 570895
Houston, Texas 77257-0895
www.bridgestolife.org

PRAISE FOR RESTORING PEACE

"*Restoring Peace* is not for sissies. It tells of perpetrators who take responsibility for their crimes and victims who face perpetrators and bare their pain and anger. The beauty of this book is that it lays out steps of the spiritual journey for us all to take. I hope *Restoring Peace* spreads like wildfire across this country."

—Sister Helen Prejean, CSJ, author of *Dead Man Walking*

"*Restoring Peace* is a marvelous book about how to really restore any broken relationship. I was amazed at the depth of this explanation of biblical truths. Reconciliation and restoration are not easy, but they are very doable if parties will follow the path laid out in this book."

—Carol Vance, former Chairman of the Board, Texas Department of Criminal Justice and author of *After the Leap*

"In *Restoring Peace*, Kirk Blackard, drawing upon his experience in a groundbreaking prison ministry, has given us a well-written, theologically sound book and a practical method for reconciling our personal relationships."

—Sam Todd, Episcopal priest and author of *An Introduction to Christianity: A first-millennium foundation for third-millennium thinkers.*

"I met John Sage as well as several of the other crime victims involved in Bridges To Life some years ago. I was moved by their stories and vision and since that time have followed Bridges

To Life's unique program with great interest. Here now is a book that not only gives us insight into how such an approach is applied in a prison setting but—as the subtitle indicates—shows all of us ways to apply those lessons in our own personal lives."

—Dr. Howard Zehr, Professor, Eastern Mennonite University and author of *Changing Lenses.*

"Kirk Blackard's very powerful and genuine writing of *Restoring Peace* is an excellent resource for therapists interested in spirituality vs. religiosity, narrative storytelling, empowerment, forgiveness, and conflict resolution."

—Dr. Lynelle Yingling, Marriage and Family Therapist, owner of J&L Human Systems Development

"The basic principles discussed in *Restoring Peace* are imperative principles for victims to heal and continue their lives as survivors and not victims. This book will be an invaluable tool in communicating these principles to anyone dealing with the aftermath of abuse."

—Deborah Mosely, Executive Director, The Bridge Over Troubled Waters, Inc.

"In *Restoring Peace*, Kirk Blackard uses the threads of loss, anger, hurt, and despair to weave a pattern for a life of purpose, self-realization, hope, faith, and love for the collective all of us."

—Raven Kazen, Director, Victim Services Division, Texas Department of Criminal Justice

****

KIRK BLACKARD is a mediator, arbitrator, and author of two books on conflict and conflict management. He lives with his wife Marcia in Houston, Texas, where he is a volunteer facilitator with Bridges To Life.

Restoring Peace

is dedicated to

the Bridges To Life victim volunteers.

—————

There can be no better role models of courage,

commitment, and unconditional love.

ACKNOWLEDGMENTS

This book, like earlier additions of Restoring Peace, is a collaborative effort. The words are mine, but the ideas and spirit are largely from others. Therefore, I have many people to acknowledge and thank.

John Sage, founder and Executive Director of the Bridges To Life prison ministry, is first on the list. John and I worked together to make the book accurately reflect the concepts and ideals of Bridges To Life and to present them in a way that benefits offenders who participate in the Bridges To Life Program. Without John Sage, the book would not have been possible.

The real heroes of *Restoring Peace* are the victim volunteers—those men and women who have suffered the worst ravages of criminal conduct and yet have chosen to use that suffering to help their fellow human beings who are serving time in Texas prisons. All combine to make Bridges To Life what it is, and no doubt all would have graciously contributed to this book in a more direct way had they been asked. Those who were asked and whose stories or contributions appear in the following pages are Jan Brown, Chris Castillo, Bob and Kathy Connell, Jesse Doiron, Tom Ferris, Connie Hilton, Paula Kurland, John Sage, and Patricia Stonestreet. They deserve special thanks.

The others who make Bridges To Life possible and who made an immeasurable contribution to this book are the offender volunteers. Since confidentiality is a critical element of the ministry, I cannot thank them by name, but they know who they are. Thanks for your help.

Several Bridges To Life volunteers also made important contributions by providing ideas, discussing issues with me, reading and criticizing drafts of the manuscript, and offering moral support. Bob Christy, Nancy Darley, Debbie Mosley, and Charles Novo provided invaluable assistance on the first edition. Charles Novo and Charlotte Mitchell did the same for this edition. Thanks for your help and support.

Fred Haman, Visitation Pastor of Christ The King Lutheran Church in Houston and a Bridges To Life volunteer facilitator; Samuel Todd, retired Episcopal priest and author of *An Introduction to Christianity*; and Dr. Lynn Mitchell, resident scholar in religion at the University of Houston graciously agreed to read all or part of the manuscript and keep me as straight as possible on the theological aspects of the Bridges To Life experience. Chaplain Fred Broussard reviewed the manuscript to insure that it accurately reflects life in the Texas Department of Criminal Justice. Evelyn Nolen and my wife, Marcia, suggested innumerable editorial changes that greatly improved the manuscript. Thanks for their input. Any mistakes that remain are mine alone.

As always, thanks to Marcia, Drew, Chris and Lisa for supporting me in all my efforts.

Victim volunteers typically join the Bridges To Life experience because they "want to help the offenders." Inevitably, however, the volunteers quickly learn that it is they who benefit and that they receive more than they give. So it is with me. I thought writing this book would help Bridges To Life and others. I now understand that I am the one receiving the most benefit. Hopefully you will receive some benefit as well. If so, thank all those acknowledged above.

Kirk Blackard

CONTENTS

1

FOREWORD

You bridged the gap and included us in it.
Inmate, Hamilton Unit

This is a revised edition of *Restoring Peace* that was originally published for the general public in 2005. Like the first edition, it starts where Bridges To Life started: with John Sage, the founder and current Executive Director of the organization. He is the author of this Foreword.

* * *

I was enthusiastic back in 2004 when Kirk Blackard first proposed writing a book about the restorative justice process called Bridges To Life, which had been very effectively used in Texas prisons. I was not certain what shape the book might take or how it would eventually be used, but my inner voice told me that it would be very positive for Bridges To Life. The first edition of the book became a centerpiece of the Bridges To Life curriculum. Thousands of copies have been printed and distributed throughout Texas and the world, and we are pleased that Kirk has authored this revised edition, primarily for incarcerated offenders.

When I founded Bridges To Life in 1998, I was not aware of the restorative justice movement. I had limited experience in volunteer work inside prisons, but that experience was so powerful that it inspired me to start Bridges To Life in order to make a difference in the lives of crime victims and offenders. At the very core of my passion for this work was the desire to keep other families from going through the years of horror that my family experienced after my sister Marilyn's brutal murder on June 30, 1993. If the program helps incarcerated offenders change their lives and not commit crimes in the future, then it has prevented innocent families from being victims of crime.

After experiencing the gut-wrenching aftermath of my sister's murder, I have great empathy with victims of crime. In Bridges To Life, we define "victim" as anyone who has been affected or had a family member or loved one affected by crime, particularly when the incident profoundly changed his or her life. Crime plunges innocent victims into a dark place they did not ask for or deserve. Victims of crime are the very heart and soul of Bridges To Life, and I see *Restoring Peace* as a tribute to the courage and character of all crime victims.

My work in prisons for many years has helped me develop empathy for offenders as well. I never excuse their offenses, but I now understand many of the influences that have led to their behavior. I am now able to condemn the behavior while recognizing the good that is in the hearts and minds of individuals who are incarcerated.

Restoring Peace provides a structure and focus for our reconciliation process that all offenders can use as a guide to making significant changes in their thinking. The journey to restore peace is much the same for all of us. At our very human core, we have a desire for peace ("shalom") in our lives. Life often interrupts or destroys that peace, and we all search for our way back, a return to the peace we knew as a young child or experienced in the good times of our lives. The journey toward peace requires radical change. It involves a transformation of heart, mind, and habits. We have witnessed this transformation in many of the offender participants during the Bridges To Life process. The recidivism statistics of our graduates relative to general population inmates indicate a very significant impact.

The principles of Bridges To Life discussed in *Restoring Peace* are both simple and complex. A "willing heart" is essential to understanding and absorbing this book. Read it slowly with an open mind and an open heart. Read the concepts, the stories, and the questions and adapt them specifically to your life. Let the book "speak to you." Our backgrounds and circumstances are so varied that one person's answer is not the same as another person's. One person may need to work more on faith, one on forgiveness, and another on repentance. By reading this book, you may be shown some answers about your life that you have never before considered.

I have spent a great deal of time pondering a quotation from Ernest Hemingway's *Farewell to Arms:* "The world breaks everyone, and afterwards, some are strong at the broken places." A significant part of my journey after Marilyn was murdered was toward becoming strong where I had been broken. For a number of years, that seemed impossible. I continued to feel broken by Marilyn's murder and other difficulties and hardships that life presented me. I continued to seek the path toward restoring my inner peace and, eventually, it led me to establish Bridges To Life. I believe that all who continue to seek will find their way to peace. It takes work, patience and persistence; and this book can be an important part of your journey toward becoming "strong at the broken places."

I want to thank the volunteers and donors who make Bridges To Life possible. Also, I want to thank and commend the offenders who have completed the Bridges To Life program in the past. I hope and pray that it was a major step for them toward restoring peace in their lives. I am grateful to the many employees of the Texas prison system who help implement this program. And many thanks to the author, Kirk Blackard, who worked with passion, persistence, and focus to complete the first edition of *Restoring Peace* and to make the changes resulting in this edition.

As a final comment, I request of you the same thing that we ask of all offenders at the beginning of each project: complete the project. Don't make lasting judgments or decisions as to what effect it had on you until you have finished. This is a total process that must be completed to have significant and lasting effect.

I pray that this book and the Bridges To Life program will be a blessing for you and your family. I applaud you for participating and ask you to complete the program and give it your best effort.

STUDY QUESTIONS
1. Why do you think John Sage founded Bridges To Life?

2

INTRODUCTION

"It's a program of tragedy and triumph."
Inmate, Beto Unit

An unspeakable horror is the starting point for this book about change, love, and peace. Two nineteen-year-olds had been cruising a Houston neighborhood for two days, looking for a car to steal to go to Bay City and party with friends. They spotted Marilyn as she was going back and forth moving clothes from the trunk of her car into her apartment. They crept silently into her home, hid in wait, and attacked her as she returned down a hall for another load of clothes. The two stabbed her with at least three different knives, pounded her on the head with a statue from a nearby sofa table, and suffocated her with a plastic bag while she begged for her life. She never had a chance.

Marilyn's brother, John Sage, received that terrible phone call later that evening, June 30, 1993, from his wife, Frances. She said, "Johnny, something horrible has happened. Marilyn's dead! Someone has killed her!"

Marilyn and John were born nineteen months apart, the fourth and fifth in a family of eight children. They were best of friends from the time they were toddlers. They played together, grew up together, went to college at Louisiana State University together, and John married Marilyn's close friend. Now Marilyn was gone, brutally murdered by a couple of teenagers who just wanted her car.

Marilyn's murderers were arrested within forty-eight hours. In the 1994 trial, the jury took less than an hour to convict the first murderer, and even less time to assess the death penalty. The second was also convicted and assessed the death penalty a year later.

But John didn't feel that anything had been fixed. He felt no better with the murderers on death row. Their conviction didn't bring his sister back, and his wonderful memories of her were forever ruined by images of the brutal murder scene. Instead, he had become a prisoner of his own rage, severe depression, and misery and had lost control of his life. John went to a therapist and started taking medication, but that wasn't enough. He also threw himself into his spiritual life as he had never done before. John prayed daily, hourly, joined a Bible study group, and learned that God loved him as much as He loved His own son. John learned that the key to receiving that love was to surrender to it once and for all. After a while his depression lifted, and he was able to go back to work, spend time with his family, and lead a stable life.

John, however, decided to do more than accept God's love and return to a life that was as normal as possible. He needed and wanted more. He wanted his life to honor Marilyn's life and decided that the best way to do so was to commit himself to reducing crime and preventing similar tragedies from happening to others. He asked himself where he could do the most to reduce crime, and concluded that it was among people who are incarcerated. He knew that many youth offenders graduate from juvenile facilities to adult prisons, and that 67 percent of all inmates who are discharged from the nation's prisons are arrested again within three years of their release. Released individuals violate the terms of their parole, hurt others, return to their old criminal ways, or otherwise commit acts that all too frequently cause them to be locked up again. They commit crimes at a much higher rate than other people.

Thus, John concluded that because so many released individuals commit more offenses, he could most effectively prevent future crime by helping change the lives of people who are currently locked up. He also thought about his own experience and concluded that people who have suffered as victims of crime are best positioned to help offenders, and that by helping offenders they could also help themselves deal with their continuing pain and hurt. His conclusions gave birth to Bridges To Life.

BRIDGES TO LIFE

John Sage founded Bridges To Life in 1998. Victims of brutal crimes—murder, rape, assault, severe spousal abuse—began going into Texas prisons to meet with inmates who committed such crimes against others. In the program, victims and offenders share their stories with one another and work together through a healing process based on teachings of the Bible. After the program is complete, the victims gain a measure of healing. The offenders change, some only a little but many into new and different human beings who are much less likely to commit new offenses than other inmates. Amazingly, people in both groups go beyond their mistrust and fear to establish a bond of peace and love.

As of the time of this writing, more than 9000 inmates have completed the program. Those who take part in Bridges To Life are all very different. They arrive with their heads and hearts in many different places: some with extreme feelings of guilt and remorse, others in denial of what they have done or of its effects; some sincere, some aiming to do a con job; some acknowledging, some blaming; some open like a butterfly, others closed like a cocoon; some with great hope, others seemingly beyond hope. But all are in search of something.

Great changes occur during the course of the program. The offenders aren't changed into someone who will never do wrong again, and some will earn another sentence. But everyone changes. Offenders, many for the first time, acknowledge what they have done and talk about its effect on others, recognize they need to forgive and also ask for forgiveness, and struggle with the tools to make peace with their loved ones and society at large. They come to see their search for peace and a better life as a never-ending journey, with the Bridges To Life experience an important step in that journey.

Those who participate in the program almost always describe how their lives have been changed for the better. And several thousand of them have now been released. Of those individuals, relatively few have been locked up again, and very, very few have returned for committing new violent crimes. Bridges To Life truly helps those with trouble in their lives turn themselves around.

In early 2009, several of us who had been working with adult prison inmates finally came to understand something that we had not seen before. We finally understood that young boys and girls who are locked up in youth facilities are very often just stopping over on their way to the big house—to an adult prison.

And we also understood that you—offending youth and adults alike—nearly always have much in common. With a few exceptions, you come from a dysfunctional or broken home. Perhaps you never knew your father and your mother deserted you. Or your father abused your mother—and you. Or your parents use drugs and often sell them to others. Or your mother is a prostitute, or one or both of your parents are themselves in prison. And you are afraid, hurt, angry—and you want to get even. You skipped out on school and used alcohol and drugs when you knew better. You joined a gang so you would have a "family." Or you did some shoplifting—or maybe sold some drugs, or perhaps committed burglary—to get what you wanted. You lashed out and hurt others—maybe even physically attacked them or murdered them. You got caught. You want to turn your life around, but you don't know how. This book is for all of you.

It's important to remember that you need to be concerned with your behavior, and not with your value as a person or your worth as one of God's children. Nelda, a forty-six-year-old former drug dealer serving five years in prison, this time for shoplifting, put it this way, as big tears flowed from her sad, red eyes: "This is my fourth time at the rodeo. I've made mistakes, but I'm not a mistake." And that's the case with you. You may have made many mistakes, but you are not a mistake. Bad behavior does not make you a bad person.

Bridges To Life recognizes that you must live with the fact that you have not behaved as you should have, or have hurt other people, or committed crimes against others. The program will not try to play God by condemning you for your mistakes. But it will address the behavior that causes your troubles.

The program also recognizes that life is a journey with many ups and downs, that people can and do change, and that a pattern of bad behavior at one stage in your life does not have to last forever. Having a misguided life as a young person does not necessarily mean a troubled life forever.

Bridges To Life will help you turn your life around. It will help you avoid committing crimes like the two nineteen year olds who murdered John Sage's sister and were sent to death row.

THE THREE PARTS OF BRIDGES TO LIFE

The three basic parts of the Bridges To Life program are belief in God, the magic of telling our stories, and the principles covered in the Bridges To Life process.

Belief in God is the foundation of Bridges To Life, even though no one will try to convert you to a particular point of view regarding religion. Bridges To Life emphasizes spirituality in the deepest sense of belonging and inclusiveness rather than any particular religious belief or set of practices. People of any faith are welcome if they have a sincere desire to improve their lives and stay out of trouble in the future. Bridges To Life simply aims to show you the transforming power of God's love and forgiveness. While the program is presented from a Christian point of view, it also works for people whose faith is not Christian. It does so because their humanity and their right to worship in their own way are respected.

Stories are the second important aspect of the Bridges To Life experience. Each participant tells his or her story in some detail during the program, and they hear stories of people whose lives have been greatly affected by crime. The speakers nearly always start by stating some facts about their lives, like completing a test in school or filling out an employment application, and often they deny certain truths about themselves as well. But soon the speakers begin to reveal who they are and how they feel. They tell of having and losing, power and weakness, being disappointed and disappointing others, love and hate, being hurt and hurting others, fear and hope. Each story is unlike the others, because each life is different. Yet, the stories show how much alike we all are, and they create relationships that help connect people with one another.

This book will share stories from the Bible, from offenders who are incarcerated, and from victims of crime. The stories will help you put your concerns in perspective and show you they can be dealt with. They will also teach you to listen and provide a model for you to use in telling your own story, the truest form of confession. The stories you will read here are not just interesting tales but are very personal accounts of how people live with pain every day: stories in which the participants rip their chests open and let people see what is inside.

The third element of the Bridges To Life experience is the process, a planned discussion among participants that explores principles that will help you deal with the trouble and conflict in your life. The primary topics of discussion include:

- Crime and Conflict
- Faith
- Stories
- Responsibility
- Accountability
- Confession
- Repentance
- Forgiveness
- Reconciliation
- Restitution

These concepts are discussed in the following chapters of this book. Participants in the Bridges To Life program will read the book and write their answers to appropriate questions in the *Bridges To Life Study Guide*. Volunteer facilitators will work with small groups to encourage honest, open discussion and steer the sessions to help you learn from one another and figure things out for yourself with God's help.

PEACE IS A JOURNEY

As you read these chapters, keep three things in mind. First, your road to peace will be a journey and not an event. You will need to visit and revisit each part, continue to think about your responsibility and accountability, confess when and to whom needed, repent by changing who you are, live a forgiving life, continue to work on your reconciliation, and make restitution as often as needed for everyone to be treated fairly. Second, while these actions are discussed in a logical order, you may choose a different one. Do what needs to be done when the spirit moves you, and don't worry about a particular sequence. And third, remember that some of the actions can be done by you alone, while others, such as reconciliation, require action by someone other than yourself. Don't feel bad, therefore, if sometimes you do your best and still don't accomplish all you would like.

Your challenge is to take the journey toward building peace with your parents, brothers and sisters, friends, and society in general. That journey starts with Chapter 3.

STUDY QUESTIONS

1. What are the three basic parts that are the essence of the Bridges to life experience?
2. What do you hope to get out of your Bridges To Life experience?
3. What personal fears or concerns do you have about participating in Bridges To Life?

3

CRIME AND CONFLICT

I thought the only one I hurt was myself, but now I know there were others.
Inmate, Allred Unit

Conflict and crime began in the Garden of Eden. Eve ate the forbidden fruit and gave some to her husband, Adam. God confronted them about their sins and the blame game began. Adam tried to avoid responsibility by blaming Eve, and he chose to hide rather than acknowledge what he had done and make excuses rather than admit the truth. Eve blamed the serpent, claiming it tricked her. We can guess that there were problems in their household, and they not only offended God but also each other. The story of conflict, hurt, and crime continued with their children. Cain was a farmer, and Abel a shepherd. At harvest time, Cain brought the Lord a gift of farm produce, while Abel brought a cut of meat from a lamb. When the Lord accepted Abel's gift but rejected Cain's, Cain became furious. Rather than address God's rejection of his offering, Cain murdered his brother. Unfortunately, misbehavior and crime have been with us ever since.

If you are locked up, it's probably because you have committed, or are suspected of having committed, one or more crimes. The primary purpose of this book is to help you deal with your situation and avoid committing a crime in the future. Therefore, we will start with a brief discussion of what crime is, what its consequences are, and what typically causes it.

CRIME

The simplest definition of crime is "behavior that violates the law." United States laws against crime have their roots in the Old Testament and the English common law. Our laws have been written to reflect the moral sense of our community—to tell us what is right and wrong as well as what the government has outlawed, and to further the social purposes for which our community exists.

In the early years of our country, crime and sin were considered very much the same, and criminal laws prohibited various kinds of religious offenses. These kinds of crimes have now been abolished, and we have full freedom of conscience as far as our religious practice is concerned and in many other areas of life. However, many types of behavior are forbidden, and the law imposes serious consequences on those who fail to live by the designated rules of our society. Those who commit crimes are subject to punishment.

As most of us know, each state, along with the federal government, has a large number of laws establishing rules for our society—laws punishing offenses against other people, property, the family and the public. The laws aim to protect individuals and society. In most cases, when the law is violated there is a clear offender and a clear victim who gets hurt in an obvious way. Someone does something against the will of another person, group of persons, or their property; and the action violates the law. For example, cases of murder, assault, or theft have a clear offender and a clear victim.

The victim and the hurt involved are not quite so clear to some people in another group of offenses. In matters such as many forms of gambling; prostitution; and possession, use, or sale of drugs the hurt and the victim are not always so obvious to everyone. The people involved generally appear to participate by their own free will, and they seem to agree to what is going on. They often argue that no one is being hurt—or if they are, it is by their own choice. Good try! We all know that the state has decided that such activities are hurtful. They, at least indirectly, hurt many individuals and they hurt society. There are laws against them. And we all know they are crimes, just like stealing, assault, and murder are crimes. The fact that some may not accept the illegality and consequences does not prevent them from being crimes.

Certain offenses can be defined as noncriminal misbehavior that is inappropriate or illegal only for children. In these cases, a youth has violated certain rules of society, but has not done something that would be illegal for an adult to do. For example, a teenager may be taken to juvenile courts or referred to child welfare agencies if he is involved in misbehavior such as running away from home, truancy, curfew violations, or underage drinking. While normally not a crime in the same sense as adult violations of criminal laws, such behavior is still "against the rules" and can lead to restrictions on the teenager who commits the offense.

THE CONSEQUENCES OF CRIME

Many of the consequences of crime are obvious, impossible to miss. Just watch the nightly news. A distraught mother or sibling talks about the horror of a child being murdered and a family that will never be the same again. A drunk driver has wiped out the father and bread-winner of a close-knit family. We see scenes of young men stealing to feed their drug habit or a Mexican border war over drug distribution and profits.

But, just as an iceberg is mostly under water and out of sight, most of the consequences of crime are not so obvious. Take the story of Julian and Jessica.

Julian is a 35 year-old who lived in Amarillo, Texas. He and his wife Sue had been married thirteen years and have two beautiful children—Patricia, age ten, and Jake, age nine. They had a good life. Julian held the same job for ten years and Sue started working part-time after the children began school. They attended church regularly and enjoyed short road trips and eating out as a family. Julian and Sue had a generally good marriage—with only a few rough spots along the way, primarily concerning how to manage their tight budget. A couple of years ago, Julian began feeling confined, that his life was passing him by. He began spending most evenings alone in his room on his computer, visiting porn sites and chat rooms.

Julian met Jessica in a computer chat room. She told him she was a twenty-three year old teacher at a local high-school, and they seemed to have a lot in common. They agreed to meet, and Julian picked her up around 11:00 am at school. They went to a local spot, had sex, and Jessica was back at school in time to attend her 1:00 pm class.

The police picked Julian up the next morning. Although Jessica had had previous sexual experience—in fact, she had a reputation all over school as being promiscuous—and was a willing partner in this encounter, she was only sixteen and Julian had hurt her feelings when he dumped her so quickly back at school. Jessica told her parents, and they filed charges for statutory rape.

Julian hired an attorney to get him off, but it didn't work. He was able to delay a decision for almost a year, but after lengthy haggling with the District Attorney's office, they entered into a plea bargain deal. Julian is now serving five years in prison and upon release will have to register with the state as a sex offender. He is angry at Jessica for lying and at himself for being so stupid. He hates prison, is fearful nearly all the time, and can't imagine what life will be as a registered sex offender after his release. But at least no one else was hurt by what he did.

Really!

The web of hurt caused by what Julian and Jessica did—in private and with full agreement of both—is almost unbelievable. Mostly, it affected their families. Every family involves many people who are connected and interconnected in numerous ways, and what one person does affects others. Think of Julian's family. His wife, Sue, was devastated and cried for days. She got counseling from her church minister, then filed for divorce. Although she has found a full-time job, she hates it and struggles to provide for her family while Julian is locked up. Both children are teased and humiliated in school because their dad is in prison. Jake particularly misses his father when no one is there for his soccer games. Both kids are depressed and are beginning to misbehave more and more. Julian's mother and father got a second mortgage on their home to help pay Julian's attorney fees and to help support their grandchildren, and now they are struggling to pay their bills. They are afraid they will lose their home. They have withdrawn from their church Bible study group because of their embarrassment. And Jessica's family…and on and on.

Such hurt and suffering from one illegal action—one crime—that both people involved in agreed to. Think of the consequences of other crimes that seem so much worse and have more obvious victims.

CAUSES OF CRIME

Discord and crime of all sorts continue today. As an offender in the Bridges To Life program you have been locked up because of your actions that violated certain rules or were crimes against another person or society as a whole—actions that have hurt other human beings and that you must live with and deal with. The purpose of Bridges To Life—and hopefully your aim as well— is to help you correct your misbehavior and avoid committing offenses again. To change your life, you need to first think about why you did what you did, because it's almost impossible to change if you don't first address the situation that caused the offending behavior. Therefore, the following sections discuss the main reasons people commit crimes

Let's start with the basics. James 4:1-3 provides the following biblical insight into what causes problems among people:

> What is causing the quarrels and fights among you? Isn't it because there is a whole army of evil desires within you? You want what you don't have, so you kill to get it. You long for what others have, and can't afford it, so you start a fight to take it away from them. And yet the reason you don't have what you want is that you don't ask God for it. And even when you do ask you don't get it because your whole aim is wrong—you want only what will give you pleasure.

With this insight in mind, let's explore some specific reasons people cause conflict and commit crimes. Experts have studied the causes of crime for years and have developed different theories. At times in the past, criminal behavior has been blamed on demonic influence, planetary influence, bumps on the head, secretion of androgen from the testes, and other discredited causes.

Even today, experts often do not agree as to why people disobey rules, hurt other people, or commit crimes. A primary reason for the disagreement is that there are many causes of misbehavior and crime, they work together in many different ways, and they lead to different kinds of actions. For example, the action of a criminally insane psychopath is driven by forces that are different from those that motivate a petty thief; driving while intoxicated has different causes than stealing.

Although the causes of conflict and criminal behavior are complex and often difficult to determine, certain situations or types of behavior, observed time and again in the Bridges To Life experience, tend to cause most of the problems we encounter on a daily basis. These causes—different perspectives, conflicting needs and wants, abuse of power and control, confusing respect with fear or envy, uncontrolled anger, and substance abuse or addiction—are discussed below. Understanding them and thinking deeply about those that affect your life will help you as you proceed through the healing process.

Different Perspectives

Our perspective has to do with what we believe and how we see the world in which we live. Our perspective is determined by many influences of our life stories—such as the lessons we learned from our parents, the way people around us live, our experiences and education, the way our brains process information, our own self-concept and expectations. Because people have different perspectives, they often view the same event or conversation and reach widely differing conclusions about what really occurred—and they often make equally differing decisions as to what is right and wrong in a particular situation.

Think about Julie. She drinks, takes pills, smokes marijuana, and uses crack cocaine because they help her forget about her problems. She has problems with friends and boyfriends, but mostly with her parents. She just can't understand why her parents sit on her like they do—why they try to tell her who to be friends with, where to go, what to do. The last time she fought with her mother she got so mad she went to her room and tried to cut the veins in her arm with a knife. Do her parents live on another planet? Well—perhaps they almost do. They grew up in the 1960s in a rural area in northeast Texas—in a lower middle-class, isolated, conservative, religious home. They have definite feelings about how Julie should behave. She should behave much like they did. Julie grew up in a middle-class area of Dallas in the 1990s. She sees the world very differently.

And think about Ronald: a thirty-two year old man, born and raised by his penniless grandmother in a Dallas slum, now incarcerated at the Beto unit. He never knew his father, knew his mother only as a prostitute and drug dealer, dropped out of school in ninth grade, ran away and began living on the street at age sixteen. All those laws that tried to tell him what he could and could not do made no sense to him. He "did what he's gotta do" to survive. So what if he ended up in prison—he would have a roof over his head and three squares each day. Is it surprising that his views are different from the people in Austin who make the laws or the police who enforce them? Is it surprising that he sold drugs and stole from others?

Our perspective often determines how we behave in a particular situation. Frequently we don't believe what we see; instead, we see what we believe. We interpret events or messages according to our own environment and beliefs. And how we interpret them affects what we do. Thus, Julie and her parents have very different perspectives—that lead to continual fights. And Ronald had few reservations about dealing drugs or stealing from others because he didn't see that he was hurting anyone except himself, while society and the police saw a great deal of damage everywhere. They passed laws against his behavior and enforced them by sending him to prison.

Think about your own situation. How does your perspective differ from that of parents, family, friends, or strangers you interact with? How does it differ from the perspective of those making and enforcing the laws we all must live under? Do you need to think more about how you view the world and consider changing your perspective?

Confusing Needs and Wants

Sometimes confusion of needs and wants causes conflict and leads to crime. Needs are what we can't do without. Physical needs would include such things as adequate food and clothing, a roof over our head, reasonable transportation, and other items necessary for our livelihood. Wants are what we desire because we like them or they make us feel better, but they are not essential to our well-being. Our wants might include a popular pair of shoes or jeans, a jazzy new car, eating at an expensive restaurant—or drugs to give us a high.

Fortunately, in America nearly all people can get what they need without violating the law. This doesn't mean it's easy or even comfortable for all of us. You no doubt know some people who have great difficulty meeting their needs. They (or their parents if they are children) have health problems, or can only find low-paying jobs, or have been laid off. They are so poor they are barely making it and have to live hand-to-mouth under very difficult circumstances. Difficult as it may be, however, most people can take care of themselves, even if sometimes they have to swallow their pride and accept help from public or private social services agencies.

One can understand the moral dilemma of the parent who as a last resort steals milk for a starving baby. The evidence suggests, however, that this type of situation is rare. Bridges To Life offenders almost never talk of crimes involving needs. They talk of wants and desires, and what they did to fulfill them. Think honestly of your own experience. Do you know of a case where a person committed theft, burglary, or another crime because doing so was necessary to meet a need—or at least to meet a need that wasn't brought about by spending on wants? Probably not.

Many needs exist because a person satisfies wants first. Think of Debra. She says she forged checks and shop-lifted items from Walmart because she needed money to pay the rent and feed her children. But her wants were the reason she was short on money. She spent too much time in bars, bought too many cigarettes, drove a car she couldn't afford, and partied so much she lost her job. She claimed her needs drove her to crime. But did they—really?

There is nothing wrong with wanting something and trying to fulfill our wants. Wanting something often provides the motivation and spark that makes life interesting, and getting what we want often leads to a better and more purposeful life. We admire the immigrant, the poor, the persecuted who want a better life and do what it takes that is legal to rise above their circumstances.

But uncontrolled want—want for improper things or want that drives us to use improper means to attain our desires—can cause us problems. It does so in two basic ways. First, we may do things that violate the law. Think of Kimberly, who shoplifted because she wanted drugs, or Derwin who stole a car because he thought he needed a more powerful one to impress his friends, or Floyd who got drunk because he wanted to relax, and then murdered a woman with his car while he was driving drunk. All are situations where the uncontrolled wants of the individuals led to behavior that was a direct violation of the law—and led each of them to prison.

The second problem with uncontrolled wants is that they often destroy relations with family or friends. A child wants money, things or freedom, and the parent cannot or will not provide them. Or two people want the same thing. Two small children want the same toy. Two men want the affection of the same woman. Two gangs want control of the same territory. How often do such conflicting wants lead to fights—and worse? Those involved may stop short of violating the law, but they often treat every want as a need. The person who sees everything as a need aims to get what he believes he needs—one way or another, and often destroys relationships and hurts others in the process.

Think honestly about your own situation and how you have behaved in the past. Have you behaved improperly or illegally in order to get what you need? Or have uncontrolled wants caused problems instead?

Abuse of Power and Control

Offenders in the Bridges To Life experience are often victims as well as offenders. They frequently have experienced a lifetime of domestic violence and emotional abuse. Their fathers abused their mothers. Their fathers, grandfathers, stepfathers, stepbrothers, or other relatives abused them, often sexually. To escape the abuse, they ran away from home at an early age— perhaps to live with relatives who also abused them. The girls took up with and married so-called knights in shining armor. Soon, the knights began abusing them. They eventually divorced and married other abusers. The stories are all very much alike. People who were supposed to love them controlled them instead.

Ramona, a thirty-five-year old inmate at the Henley unit described a particularly brutal case. She explained, hesitantly at first but then in a flood of emotions, that she took up with a drug-addicted truck driver whom she knew to be controlling, married him shortly thereafter, and lived in a nightmare of intimidation and abuse. Her husband beat her severely on an occasion when she was three months pregnant, saying she didn't bring him enough drugs to satisfy his appetite. He then forced her to go to bed when he did so he wouldn't have to sleep alone. After her husband was asleep, Ramona slipped out of bed to watch TV. A couple of hours later a dreadful pain hit. She was afraid to wake her husband because he would beat her for disturbing his sleep. She eventually went to the bathroom, delivered a dead baby in the bathtub, and flushed it down the commode. The next morning she was barely able to stand when her husband forced her to cook his breakfast. He finally took her to a hospital but beat her again when she got blood on the velour seats of his car.

People like Ramona—boys and girls, men and women who are subjected to domestic abuse see the worst of the abuse of power and control—actual or threatened physical harm, sexual assault, intimidation, name-calling and put-downs, unreasonable withholding of money, public or private ridicule and humiliation, continual criticism, and other harmful behavior.

Less forceful use of power may also cause problems. Inappropriate use of power often occurs when one controls or dominates another in lesser ways—when one person uses pressure to get another to do or not do what the controller wants; when the controller must have his or her own way, have the last word, be seen as always right, in effect own the other person; or when the controller wants to have the other person live by his or her standards. Some examples are parents who pressure their daughter to be a "Barbie Doll" instead of the person the daughter wants to be, a husband who consistently complains about his wife's dress, or a friend who always insists on going to his favorite restaurant.

A controlling person easily rationalizes or explains away her behavior. She believes she knows more about the other person's inner reality—his wants, needs, and desires—than he does. Or she thinks her actions are necessary and right as a parent, spouse, friend, or other person in a relationship. Or the controlling person believes the other person deserves the treatment, or equates control with love, and fools herself into believing she is acting out of love.

The fact is, however, that those who are violently abused or controlled in lesser ways are all victims, and the controller is the victimizer. The controller sees the victim as an object, not as another human being. The only way the controller can get power and a sense of worth is to victimize. If he attacks or rapes or molests or otherwise controls someone, he no longer feels weak. He is in charge.

Surprisingly, however, the more a person tries to control, the more he loses control and risks destroying the only thing he has with the other person that allows him to meet both their needs—

their relationship. Even the lesser types of controlling nearly always cause problems and have unintended consequences that are the opposite of what the controller wants. Too much control can cause arguments and unacceptable behavior when the other person resists. Being too controlling can also have long-term negative effects. It makes the other person feel "erased," as though she does not exist as an individual person, robs her of her self-confidence and ability to make reasonable choices, and tends to create a robot rather than a vibrant, creative human. Too much control makes real love difficult. It's hard to love someone who continually wants to control and change you.

To make matters worse, problems of power and control often run in cycles. From generation to generation, the sins of the parents are passed to the children. And the victim-victimizer cycle is at the heart of violent crime. It is difficult for boys and girls who have been abused and had their spirits imprisoned in their own homes to develop compassion and empathy. So the victim becomes the victimizer, continuing a never ending cycle of hurt and crime.

Thus, inappropriate use of power to control another person happens in a wide range of circumstances—from the evil of domestic violence and abuse to the lesser annoyances of the know-it-all who refuses to listen and always wants his way. The severity of the consequent pain also varies, but it's always there. Have you been victimized by someone who wanted to control you? Have you victimized another by trying to control him or her? How can you stop the cycle of victimization?

Confusing Respect with Fear or Envy

A man is beaten to death by two friends because he failed to pay for their meal as he had promised. One dude fails to pay a five dollar gambling debt and the other stabs him. One person thinks another stole his pocket knife, so he beats him up and later discovers the knife was only misplaced. A prison riot breaks out when one inmate changes the television channel. Are some of the fights you have seen, or perhaps been involved in, like these? Why do people become violent over such small things? Why do they want what they do not need—and commit crimes to get what they want. A gold necklace or a Rolex watch? A particular brand of clothes or shoes? A hot car? A "bad" girl? What's going on here?

Some people say it all boils down to a question of respect. They believe not paying for the meal as promised, or reneging on a gambling debt, or taking a knife, or changing the channel shows disrespect. If you believe this way, and you can't put up with the disrespect, you may do to another person what you think he deserves and expect that next time he will show you "respect." Or you "respect" the dude who is on top of his game and seems to have such a glamorous life—the one with the gold necklace, the big car, the bad girl, and all the drugs he wants for himself and his friends. You do what it takes to have what he has, to be like him. The bottom line in both cases is that you want to be "respected," and may fight, steal, sell drugs, join a gang, or do whatever else is needed to gain that respect.

But is this really the way things work? What is respect, anyway? True respect is admiring or holding esteem for an individual because of his worth or excellence as a person. Respect has great importance in everyday life. Most of us have been taught to respect our parents, teachers, older people, rules, family and cultural traditions, other people's feelings and rights, and other things that are important to a good and peaceful society.

Importantly, respect cannot be demanded or forced, though sometimes people mistakenly believe that it can. Respect is something that is earned. One earns another's respect by voluntarily doing things that show respect. It's like a boomerang. What you send out will come back to you. You can show respect to others and they will show respect to you. You can also disrespect another, and this will earn disrespect for you. In some situations you may learn that the price of disrespect is very high: "Diss me, and you suffer."

Let's look more closely at two important aspects of true respect. First, respect involves admiring or holding esteem for another as an act of free will. You cannot force someone to respect you and another person cannot force you to respect him. It is a belief, and not an action. However, respect can be shown through behavior, as we can act in ways considered respectful. On a practical level this includes giving worth and value to someone's feelings, needs, thoughts, ideas, wishes and preferences by acknowledging him, listening to him, being truthful with him, trusting him, and accepting him as an individual, unique person of value.

Second, true respect involves admiring worth or excellence as a unique human being. It recognizes the good and the honorable in a person, and it does not mean giving in to another's physical threats or being influenced by another's money or social status. The fact that one person gives in to another does not mean she respects him.

Think about what so often passes as respect in many of our lives. Perhaps one person "respects" a bigger, meaner person, or a person with a reputation as a fighter, or a person with a gun, or a person with a gang behind him. When a dude is asked why he carries a gun, he replies: "Before I had this gun, I didn't get no respect. Now I do." Or one person wants the kind of things a big-time drug dealer has—not because he respects the dealer as a person but because he wants what he has or is jealous of his status among his friends.

This is fear and envy, not respect. Fear and envy are poisonous and tear us down, while respect builds us up. Fear is life-threatening, but respect makes life better. Fear is forced, respect is earned. Envy is self centered, while respect is a positive focus on another. We learn to fear and envy, but we earn respect.

Respect and self-respect are deeply connected. Self-respect is often defined as a sense of worth or as due respect for one's self. It includes self-esteem, self-confidence, dignity, self-love, a sense of honor, self-reliance, and pride. It is the opposite of shame, putting one's self down, arrogance, and self-importance.

It is very difficult to respect others if we don't respect ourselves, and to respect ourselves if others don't respect us. A person who wants true respect lives as an honorable human being with the hope that others will voluntarily come to admire her. How this goes depends on whether she respects herself.

The value of self-respect may be taken for granted. We may discover how very important it is, though, when our self-respect is threatened, or we lose it and have to work to regain it, or when we struggle to develop or maintain it in a difficult environment. Some people find that being able to respect themselves is what matters most about avoiding bad behavior and getting their life together.

Confusing respect with fear or envy causes many problems, while having self-respect and truly respecting others fosters peace. A person who truly respects another does so because she sees her as an honorable human being—not someone she is afraid of or envies because of what she has or how others see her in society. She wants to be like the person she respects, and this means she wants to be an honorable human being. She doesn't have to cause problems to get or show respect, and her life fosters peace.

On the other hand, demanding something from another through fear fosters conflict, fights, and criminal behavior. And a person who wants what another has or wants to be seen as another is seen in society will often do what is necessary to get what she wants. This approach to life also fosters conflict, fights, and criminal behavior.

Have you ever confused respect with fear or envy? Perhaps you flew off the handle or hurt someone when you claimed he didn't show you respect—where the truth is he didn't fear you enough to submit to your control and behave as you wanted him to? Or have you done things that are wrong or illegal because you wanted to be like someone who in reality did not deserve your respect?

When we claim someone does not respect us, we need to look closely at our self and decide whether the real truth is that we don't respect our self.

Uncontrolled Anger

Lawrence decided to confront his friend and partner when he discovered the man was stealing money from the business. They went to a local park to talk in private. They argued heatedly and emotions got hotter and hotter. Lawrence's anger got the best of him, and he went to his truck, got his twenty-two-caliber pistol, and killed his friend. Lawrence is now serving twenty-five years in the Walls unit in Huntsville, along with many other men who failed to control their anger.

Mickey had been terribly abused by his father and served twenty-one years for attempted murder and other offenses. He had a terrible anger and rage problem, and on one occasion he used large spikes to nail a man who had raped his girlfriend to a picnic table.

Everybody gets angry once in a while, and feeling anger is okay, sometimes even helpful. It often tells us when we have issues we need to think about and motivates us to fix bad situations and make changes that will improve our lives and relationships. If we have a healthy approach to anger, we do what we can to address its cause and get on with our life. What better example of the positive potential of anger than John Sage. John was very angry after Marilyn was murdered. He was angry at the world, at God, at himself, and particularly at her murderers. He wanted to get a gun and blow them away. Instead, he founded Bridges To Life.

Uncontrolled, continuing anger is a different animal. Such anger is evidenced when a person sees problems everywhere, reacts to them with anger rather than as matters to be solved, behaves offensively, or fails to address his own concerns and emotions. Uncontrolled anger destroys families and other relationships, gets people fired from jobs, alienates friends, degrades personalities, fills people with shame, and causes physical diseases and disability. It also can be the first step toward violent behavior, and, as Lawrence's and Mickey's stories illustrate, cause crime and imprisonment.

Why did Lawrence get so angry that he shot and killed his best friend, and why did Mickey get so angry he nailed a person to a table? We really don't know. Predictably, however, those who cannot control their anger come from angry families, where anger is normal and expected, where no one listens until anger surfaces, and where family members don't communicate but instead try to solve problems with threats and power. For them, anger becomes a habit, a routine, an automatic response to almost any difficult situation.

Regardless of their family environment, some people express anger because it seems to serve them well. Anger seems to give people power and control, because it often intimidates others. Being angry allows one to avoid responsibility by blaming bad situations on another person. Anger protects one from other emotions, because we don't have to deal with love, caring, fear, sadness, and other emotions if we cover them with anger.

Unfortunately, anger can easily become a bigger and bigger problem when one person responds to another person's behavior, perhaps with an even stronger action. Anger is met with anger, threats are met with threats, and use of power is met with power. The first actions set the tone, and unless one person breaks the sequence, conflict grows through cycles of increasingly serious behavior. "Burn my hut, I'll burn your village."

One can guess that Lawrence's murder of his friend occurred this way. The two disagreed and then argued. Lawrence got mad and said something offensive. His friend referred to Lawrence in a way that suggested his mother was never married to his father. Lawrence shoved his friend. His friend threatened Lawrence. Lawrence shot him and ended up in prison. The cycle of anger continued.

We all face similar problems when we act out of uncontrolled anger, and spouses, family members, friends, or acquaintances respond to us and one another in increasing cycles of anger.

Substance Abuse and Addiction

Bridges To Life offenders tell many stories—of being incarcerated for forgery, shoplifting, computer fraud, possession of a controlled substance, manufacturing and sale of methamphetamines, DWI, burglary, assault with a deadly weapon, child abuse, and murder. Notwithstanding the variation in their charged offenses, offenders' stories, with few exceptions, have two common themes: they were motivated or affected by alcohol, illegal drugs, or both during the time of their offense, and, with only slightly less consistency, they grew up in families affected by alcohol, illegal drugs, or both.

These observations raise several questions. Were certain offenders predisposed to using alcohol and drugs? If so, did their predisposition arise from their genes or their environment? Did their distorted thinking cause an addiction, or did an addiction cause their distorted thinking? Did their behavior cause an addiction, or did an addiction cause their behavior? Did an addiction create the behavior or make it worse? These are complex questions, as cause and effect cannot easily be determined. Many offenders have been caught up in cycles of addiction and bad behavior, and trying to tell which is cause and which is effect is like trying to decide which came first, the chicken or the egg.

Whatever the case, it's clear that alcohol and drugs are so closely associated with criminal activity and much other conflict and bad behavior that they have to be considered as one of the primary causes. They make people too sensitive and confuse their view of reality. They make them try to manipulate and control people. They make them feel shame—and uncontrolled anger.

Think about the many ways in which alcohol and drugs affect people. Do you ever behave like this? Would you like to live with such a person? Isn't conflict predictable and understandable if one person in a relationship thinks and acts like an addict—because he is controlled by alcohol and drugs?

STUDY QUESTIONS
1. Define crime in your own words.
2. What are some kinds of harm that crime brings?
3. List several situations where someone has offended or hurt you. How did you feel on each occasion?
4. How do different perspectives (points of view, backgrounds, etc.) lead to crime, conflict, or pain?
5. Describe the difference between a need and a want.
6. Describe a situation where someone tried to control you or you tried to control someone and problems resulted.

7. What is the difference between respect and fear or envy?
8. How has anger affected your life?

4

FAITH

"First, I want to give all the glory to God."
Inmate, Kyle Unit

The Hebrews, descendants of Abraham, were new in Egypt: wanderers, shepherds, generally considered uncultured, less intelligent, and lower in status than the Egyptians. Their population grew quickly, however, and they began to threaten Pharaoh. To prevent them from gaining the upper hand, he made them slaves and put them under brutal taskmasters who made them work long and hard in the fields or carry heavy loads of brick and mortar. The Hebrews groaned beneath their burdens and wept bitterly before God, but the more they were beat down, the more they seemed to multiply. God recognized their burdens and decided to deliver them from slavery to a land "flowing with milk and honey." He selected Moses to lead them from their hard work and humiliation, and imposed many devastating plagues—turning the river to blood, frogs, lice, flies, livestock dying, boils, hail, locusts, darkness—on the Egyptians to cause Pharaoh to let them leave.

Although Pharaoh promised they could go, when they started their trek out of Egypt he chased after the Hebrews with 600 chariots driven by Egyptian officers. When the people of Israel saw the approaching Egyptian army coming after them, they were frightened and cried out to God to help them and began blaming Moses for their situation. Moses told the people that everything would be okay. They should just stand and watch, as "The Lord will fight for you, and you won't need to lift a finger." But the Lord said to Moses, "Quit praying and get the people moving!" God then opened a path through the Red Sea, dried the sea bottom, and the people of Israel walked through to the other side, while the Egyptians behind them were drowned by the returning water.

This story from Exodus demonstrates a key part of the Bridges To Life experience and suggests how we should deal with our own problems. The people of Israel were required to do their part—God told Moses to quit praying and get the people moving—but they also needed God to open the sea and provide a path. Similarly, we must do our part to improve our situation, but we also need God's help.

Belief in God is critical to success in the Bridges To Life experience: it is like the foundation of a house—absolutely essential, though not visible. Victims and offenders alike credit God with getting them through the traumas in their lives. Victims credit God with carrying them through the fear, hurt, and sorrow of losing loved ones to unspeakable horror: of having their family wiped out by a drunken driver, being abused beyond belief, having a child murdered, or other extreme victimization. Offenders who have changed their lives credit God with carrying them through the cynicism and fear of their largely wasted, sinful lives and the shame, humiliation, and hopelessness of their incarceration. One Bridges To Life volunteer said, "If you are in deep enough, only God can pull you out." And Jesus said in Mark 9:23, "Anything is possible if you have faith." (Mark 9:23)

Faith in God works in four important ways: belief in God lays down a great moral code that sets the standard for your life, it offers hope for attaining that life, it demonstrates the total, never ending love that all of us need to give and receive if we are to have peace, and it offers a process for changing to a better life. Each of these will be discussed below.

A GREAT MORAL CODE

Jack was never exposed in any meaningful way to a moral law. He was never taught right and wrong, and all his role models led him down the wrong path. Jack was born in a Dallas slum, the third child of an unmarried prostitute. He didn't know his father and his mother wasn't even sure who his father was. His father figure was "uncle Bledso," his mother's abusive, drug-dealing, live-in boyfriend. Jack began smoking a few joints with his friends at age eleven and was earning money delivering drugs at age thirteen. Although he was sent to a youth facility operated by the county to "get fixed," he was addicted by fifteen and stealing cars a year later. Now, at age twenty-two, he is locked up for the third time. He is a mean looking dude, with a slick, bald head, muscular arms and neck, and tattoos that the long-sleeved prison whites do not cover. He knows that he violated some laws, but his arrogant air suggests that he has not accepted the fact that he really did anything wrong. He behaved by the standards of his world and "did what he had to do." Jack's life has no purpose, and he has no moral compass to enable him to distinguish right from wrong, help him think about a better life, or motivate him to change his behavior and outlook.

Believing in God and aiming to do His will would offer Jack a practical moral compass for improving his behavior and mending relationships with his victims, his family, and society. The Bible describes the type of life he needs to lead in order to avoid past mistakes, pain, and suffering. It establishes standards of right and wrong, good and bad, and will provide a goal for him to shoot for and guidance in his choices.

Three great Bible codes will provide this important guidance for your life:

- The Ten Commandments: One of the Bible's great moral codes, or blueprints for living, arose as a continuation of the story of God saving Israel from the Egyptians. He promised these descendants of Abraham that He would bless and care for them and make them into a great nation, and they promised to obey Him. But the good intentions of the people quickly wore off, so God issued the "Ten Commandments," to lead them to a life of practical holiness. He demanded that the people worship no other gods than Him, refrain from making idols or taking his name in vain, and observe the Sabbath as a holy day. He also required them to honor their parents and avoid murder, adultery, stealing, lying, and envy. (Exodus 20)

- The Sermon on the Mount: In the Sermon on the Mount, Jesus demands righteousness in our hearts as well as in our deeds. Thus, for example, we are taught not only to avoid murder but also to avoid anger; not to commit adultery, but also not to look lustfully on another; to turn the other cheek when someone hits us, and other great teachings that help us address our inner beings as well as our behavior. (Matthew 5)

- The Golden Rule: Jesus' teachings often demand a good and positive life that honors others and avoids the hurt many of us so often feel or impose on others. These teachings are perhaps best reflected in what we commonly refer to as the "Golden Rule"— "Do for others what you want them to do for you." (Matthew 7:12)

Think about the Ten Commandments, the Sermon on the Mount, and the Golden Rule. These three great codes are brought together by the great commandment of Matthew 22: 37-39, "Love the Lord your God with all your heart, soul, and mind. This is the first and greatest commandment. The second most important is similar: Love your neighbor as much as you love yourself."

If Jack had loved God and his neighbor, would he have victimized society and been incarcerated? If he comes to understand and believe the three great moral codes, is he less likely to return to prison? If you followed these commandments, how often would you hurt a parent, relative, or friend; or do something that violates the law? How much more peaceful would your life be? What kind of person would you be? Just these few short verses of Exodus and Matthew provide a meaningful code for living a life that serves Him and our fellow man.

HOPE

Hope is our quiet, never ending dream for the future. When our present situation is not enough to satisfy our souls completely, no matter how good or bad, we hunger for more. And our unsatisfied search for more is the basis of biblical hope. Hope is not just a wish or want, but is real faith regarding the future. Our faith helps us see God working in our past, see our life as it is, and know that He will work in our lives in the future.

Think of two women. One is continually abused by her common law husband, and the other has been diagnosed with cancer. The first says, "I hope my husband doesn't beat me anymore. The second says, "I hope to beat this cancer." Which has true hope? The one who is being abused has only a wish. She has no real faith and is doing nothing to help God work in her life. The woman with cancer prays to God and seeks medical help. She has true hope.

Basing hope for the future on our experiences of the past seems silly for many of us. How do we use our troubles of the past to hope for a better life, especially if we are locked up in a detention facility or prison? Second Corinthians tells us the story of Paul, who faced a similar situation. Paul wrote to the church at Corinth and told the people about his hard time when he went through Asia: crushed, overwhelmed, and fearful that he would never live through it. He wrote, "We felt we were doomed to die and saw how powerless we were to help ourselves; but that was good, for then we put everything into the hands of God, who alone could save us, for he can even raise the dead. And he did help us, and saved us from a terrible death; yes, and we expect Him to do it again and again. (2 Corinthians 1: 9-10)

When you put your life in the hands of God, you receive hope. We all have problems, and no one is immune from suffering, from hurting others, from being hurt by others, from broken relationships. However, through faith in God we can make the best of our bad situation and hope for a better future. Think of John Sage's story. Good came from unspeakable horror, as he has devoted himself to people like the very criminals who murdered his sister. He shares his hope, and it multiplies.

Three influences work to give you hope. First, struggles cause us to pray, and prayer gives us hope. When we pray to God we open our mind to Him and help several elements in the healing process work together to give us hope. We typically ask for help when we pray. In doing so, we acknowledge our weaknesses and accept that we are not all-powerful and that we need help from God. We acknowledge our belief that His power is boundless and limitless. Believing this means that we also believe anything is possible, even forgiveness from someone we have hurt or reconciliation with someone who has no rational reason to reconnect with us. Furthermore, prayer helps us construct a mental image of what can be. We picture success and construct a vision of what our hope really is. When we do this, we believe more strongly and work harder and more intelligently, often in many very small ways, to do our part in making our hopes a reality.

The second influence for hope is that faith in God fosters an early success in the healing process. Most of us have not only hurt our fellow human beings but also have sinned against God. Our bad treatment of parents, brothers or sisters; our alcohol and drug use; our fighting; our thefts, burglaries, assaults, or murders; or our other offenses all violate God's commandments. But all we have to do to heal our relationship with God is to ask. And when we do so and work our God problems out, we have a success. We have mended an important relationship and seen evidence that doing so is possible. While a hearing, loving, forgiving God is easier to deal with than a hurt, abused human being, mending a relationship with God suggests that mending broken relationships is possible. Doing so gives us hope.

The third influence for hope is that God is constant, and if we believe in Him we know that He will be with us through the ups and downs. We often are scared and lonely, but a belief in God means that He is there inside us and not afraid to deal with our loss. Healing relationships with fellow human beings is rarely easy, and there will usually be good times and bad. But God is always present and never changes. We can depend on Him and rely on Him for strength when times are tough, and this gives us hope.

The words of Jobe seem to bring it all together. When he was eighteen, Jobe was involved in a burglary—and to his surprise an accomplice murdered a person. Although Jobe didn't do the killing, he was convicted of the offense. He has now served twenty-four years in the Texas prison system. Jobe is a muscular six feet, three inches tall, and looks like the athlete he was. Even today, at age 42, he looks like he could play tight end for the Houston Texans. Jobe explains biblical hope this way: "When I first got here, I believed in God but I had no connection with Him. Prison was vicious—a scary and rough situation—and I didn't understand how He would carry me. I saw no light at the end of the tunnel. Over time, I read the Bible and prayed for a real connection with God. Gradually, I calmed down, more honestly assessed my life, and learned to not worry about what I could not control. God carried me through, and this has given me hope."

LOVE

Some people question God's love because they have grown up in loveless environments. Karen is a perfect example. She grew up in Dallas, and remembers only betrayal rather than love. Her parents fought continually before her father moved out. Her stepfather pretended to love her at first, but the attention quickly became sexual abuse, while her mother looked the other way and pretended not to see the obvious. Her brother, who claimed to want to help her, got her out of the house, introduced her to drugs, and pressured her into his drug trade. She started dating an older dude who abuses her and continually cheats on her. She is now afraid she is pregnant, the older dude claims another man is the father, and Karen can't figure how to support a baby. Everyone who should love her has betrayed her, and she doesn't feel at all lovable. It's not surprising if she believes that God has betrayed her as well. One wonders how she can love when she has never really experienced love.

Or as James, a sixteen year old now serving time in a Brazoria County youth facility, said, "No one ever told me they loved me. Or if they did, it was because I had something they wanted."

The lives of Karen and James show how difficult love can be at times. But, no matter the difficulty, peace and reconciliation will not happen without love of one another and of God. A great moral standard and faith-based hope for the future are hollow without love. But love can work despite difficulty, pain, and alienation.

There are two types of love in all of us. One, need-love, is a reflection of our physical, emotional, intellectual, and other needs. It is the love that sends a lonely or frightened child to its mother's arms. Need-love is more than a selfish desire to be loved but instead is the basis of a person's spiritual life and love for God. Need-love recognizes that we are incomplete and often hurting, that our whole being is one of great need. This longing leads us to ask for God's forgiveness or support in our troubles.

Need-love leads people who are spiritually isolated and lonely to yearn for affection from their families, loved ones, and others. Regardless of how unlovable your behavior has been, you can seek love with the certainty that God will love you and with the hope that others will do so as well.

Our need for love from others motivates us to improve our lives, because we want to please someone who loves us—our parents, siblings, friends, or our God. If we accept that God loves us, we want to please Him by living the type of life He wants. We think about our lives and faults, focus on what we want to change, and make a real effort to change in order to please the ones we love and who love us.

Gift-love is God Himself working through a person. It is goodness and a Christian life exhibited in a relationship with another. Examples are the love that our parents have for us even when we have violated their trust and caused them big problems; or the love a child has for a father even though the father is mostly absent. Gift love has three important characteristics.

First, someone showing gift love often shows love to the unlovable. Many of us have done bad stuff: rebellion, lying, drugs, stealing, fighting, and such. But we are also God's creatures, each with our own special story and humanity, and in most cases our own corner of good. Those showing gift love look beyond our faults and show us love.

Second, those showing gift love often engage in a risky love. They give their hearts to people who have little experience with love and a very poor track record, which is a recipe for betrayal and distress. Loving someone without a track record is like lending all your money to a stranger. It's not a safe investment. Unlike lending money, however, the more love we give, the more we have. Loving another who may betray us is like God's love for us. He knows we will let Him down, but He loves us anyway.

Third, gift love only desires what is best for the other person. It has no agenda and expects nothing in return. It's just that loving another person is loving God, or as Jesus said in Matthew 25:40, "When you did it to these my brothers you were doing it to me!"

These lessons can be summarized as follows:

- We all need the love of God and of one another, and it's fair to say that we also want their love.
- God loves us even though we do not deserve it, and we should love others even if they have not behaved as lovable creatures. Another person's behavior—no matter how bad we think it is—should not prevent us from loving that person.
- Love is risky, but we should dare to be vulnerable and give our love. Sometimes we will be betrayed, as Christ was, but that is a risk we must take.
- We cannot love as God does if we have our own agenda. We should want what's best for the one we love.

The prayer of St. Francis of Assisi summarizes our discussion of love and sets the stage for future chapters.

O Divine Master,
Grant that I may not so much seek to be consoled as
to console;
To be understood as to understand;
To be loved as to love;
For it is in giving that we receive;
It is in pardoning that we are pardoned;
And it is in dying that we are born to eternal life.

A PROCESS FOR CHANGE

Rolando, serving fifteen years for aggravated assault, eloquently explained why he wants to change: "Nights are the worst. The dark, the quiet, the fear—it makes you think. One night I was laying in my bunk, zoned out, when three questions popped into my mind. Do you know who you were? Do you know who you are now? Do you know who you could be? Then I got a letter from a young nephew. I could tell he looked up to me and wanted to be like me. He was looking at the person he wanted to be—but I was not that person. And I could see my nephew becoming me. I had to change."

Assume that, like Rolando, you want to change your life. You can never comply fully with the Bible's moral codes, but you can accept biblical teachings as your spiritual and moral guides, sincerely want to make amends for things you have done, and hope for a positive, fulfilling life. How can you change yourself, and how do you address behavior in your past that has been wrong or hurtful? How do you restore peace in your relationships, which nearly always requires other people to change as well?

Fortunately, God's teachings guide us as we deal with our past and change our future. Just as God provides a moral compass and ultimate goal that shows us a better way for our lives, He also provides a road map for changing our lives and relationships. This guidance is the basis of the Bridges To Life experience and will be discussed in some detail in future chapters.

A journey of change based on God's teachings is the road map for the remainder of *Restoring Peace*. The starting point of the journey is your personal story. Telling your story will help you see where you are in your life and think about where you need to be. Then, in another of God's miracles, you will benefit from a biblical process for change. The process—responsibility, accountability, confession, repentance, forgiveness, reconciliation, and restitution—will be more fully developed in future chapters. This change process is a difficult journey, one that most Bridges To Life participants cannot take alone. You will need help and encouragement, which God also will provide.

STUDY QUESTIONS

1. This chapter discussed the Ten Commandments, the Sermon on the Mount, and the Golden Rule as great moral codes. What other code or codes are important to you? What "negative" codes have affected your life?

2. How does "the Great Commandment" of Matthew 22:37-39 combine the codes of the Ten Commandments and the Sermon on the Mount?

3. How has your life measured up against these codes?

4. How did question 3 make you feel? If it wasn't a good feeling, what do you need to do to change your feeling?

5. What does "hope" mean to you and why is it important?

6. What gives you hope?

7. What qualities in a person describe the kind of love you would like to experience?

5

STORIES

"I finally told my story. I got a lot out of it. My freedom."
Inmate, Hutchins Unit

Connie Hilton and her husband, George, were loving their new life together. Their children were grown and gone from home, and they could do what they wanted. They sold their house in Mesquite, moved to their dream home in the country, and began doing the things they loved. They fished, camped, hunted, took long walks, worked in their garden, talked, and just enjoyed the slow country life. Their dreams were coming true—until the night of September 16.

In the early morning hours, Connie turned to step out of her bathroom and saw a man standing in the hallway with a shotgun. She immediately screamed, and George came running. The man shot and killed him. Two others quickly joined the attacker. The three of them beat Connie until she could no longer scream or move. One of the men raped her while the other two helped themselves to the couple's possessions. They then blindfolded her, tied her up, and left her for dead.

Connie's life became a living hell. After release from the hospital, she moved in with her parents because she needed constant care and could not face staying in her house, the scene of this terrible crime. She felt numb, frozen in the past, tortured with questions she couldn't answer and accusations she made against herself that she couldn't deal with. Friends and family tried to comfort her, but she withdrew. She couldn't sleep, and the most basic aspects of life, like eating or bathing, became almost impossible tasks. Her savings disappeared, and she lost her job. She became so weak that her sister had to spoon feed her. She wanted to die.

At her low point, Connie found professional help and little by little began to restore some of her life and think about the future. She closely followed the court proceedings against her attackers. In doing so, Connie became convinced that crime victims were not being treated right by "the system," so she began working for victims' rights. As part of that work, Connie told her story for the first time.

Telling her story was difficult and heartbreaking, because it forced Connie to relive in great detail that horrible night. But it also gave her a powerful sense of release, as if by facing her ordeal she was able to take the first step toward letting go of it. Connie still suffers daily from the tragedy of that horrible night, but she has moved on with her life and become the Northeast Texas Regional Coordinator for Bridges To Life. She has devoted her life to listening to the stories of other victims of crime and to the stories of offenders who commit such crimes. She is using the power of stories to help both groups deal with the demons that haunt them.

Stories are the second important element of the Bridges To Life experience (after faith in God) and the subject of this chapter. You will learn how to tell your story and why telling it is so important to your healing process.

BRIDGES TO LIFE STORIES

The Bridges To Life experience requires each participant to tell his story in a small group at some time during the process. Telling your story may be difficult at first. But you have to open up and tell it like you were writing a play or a song or doing a rap—with you as the main character.

Your story includes talking about where they were born and lived, a little about your parents, the names and ages of your siblings, where you went to school, and other factual stuff. But the important part of your story goes far beyond the facts. You will talk about important events in your life, why things happened as they did, how you have been hurt and how you have hurt others, your beliefs and feelings, your vulnerabilities, your loneliness and isolation, your relationships with others, your dreams and hopes: information that reveals who you are as well as what you have done.

Carrie, an inmate at the Henley facility for women in southeast Texas, tells of her drug-addicted mother who loved and favored her brothers but hated her, and of her feelings of fear, loneliness, and isolation when she was locked up in a juvenile facility as a teenager. Carrie describes her feeling of loss and betrayal when her father got himself shot in a bar fight, her fear of her abusive husband, her drug use, forgery, and shoplifting, her belief that no one loved her because she was not lovable, her suicide attempts, her attempts to change, and her dream of becoming a better mother than hers had been.

Tom Ferris, whose brother was murdered by someone he thought was a friend, tells of the agony of wondering what had happened to his brother when he disappeared, of the struggle to get law enforcement to investigate, of anger and rage at the murderer's trial, of the disappointment at the light sentence the murderer received, of the never ending worry about not finding his brother's body, of the hope that someday he will be able to move on.

Other members of your Bridges To Life small group will listen and occasionally ask questions to clarify, encourage, and sometimes challenge you to be honest and tell your story like it is, without reservation. Listening is their gift of their time and attention to you. This gift shows your importance and will help you realize you are not alone in your suffering. It will help you listen to yourself and make your own judgment about who you are.

Sometimes you will have trouble remembering or focusing on important things in your life. However, when you hear others' stories the things you forget—the gaps between the events, feelings, and circumstances that you can remember—will be filled in to form a more complete picture of your life. This will give you a whole that you can examine, criticize, think about—and change if you are willing to make the effort.

Jose is a good example. He was the child of a single mother, never knew his dad, started using drugs at age twelve, was bounced among relatives, foster homes and institutions for most of his life, and is currently in prison on a ten-year sentence for dealing drugs. He tells his story with almost no emotion, acknowledging he was a drug dealer but never acknowledging or accepting responsibility for hurting anyone, except possibly himself. He sees himself as the only real victim of his story. When he hears the story of a woman whose daughter was murdered by someone burglarizing her home to buy drugs, Jose rethinks the meaning of his life and brings it into focus in a way that he can see the whole as well as the details. He now sees that he supported other dealers who sold to others, who robbed and burglarized, and perhaps killed someone's daughter. When Jose saw his life as a whole, he opened the doors to changing it.

The focus that stories bring helps us think about our lives, sort out who we are, and see the good as well as the bad. Who we are usually depends on which story is more important and true in our minds. Jane, a convicted felon serving fifteen years in prison, can tell the story of being sexually and physically abused by her stepfather, stepbrother, boyfriend, and common-law husband. She can also tell of using drugs, stealing, and gang membership—of crying daily and not wanting to live or feeling she deserved to live. Or she can tell of her spiritual conversion, rebirth, and hopes for the future. While she must acknowledge that she is the product of all her stories, she can accept the one that is her at the present time. From her viewpoint, that is who she is. Few stories end in disaster or chaos, as good usually wins out over bad. Telling about our lives helps us see and focus on the good, the possibilities, and the hope.

Each person in a Bridges To Life group tells his story in his own way without being judged, abandoned, or criticized; and each person has equal wisdom with regard to what matters at the time. The stories show participants how you are alike in so many ways. And seeing that you are so much alike helps you deal with the isolation you feel, make friends, and connect with one another in a community of human beings. Sharing experiences helps all of you remember your common humanity and appreciate that you are God's creatures, engulfed by His love.

Your stories will reveal suffering—physical, emotional, spiritual—and describe how the teller copes with that suffering. The stories have no beginning and no end, which helps you understand that certain of life's events cannot be put behind, but will be present as long as you live. The good news is that revealing the suffering and accepting that some things cannot be changed sets the stage for healing. Acknowledging past suffering sets in motion your will to find a better life and avoid the mistakes of the past.

Each story also recounts times of happiness and well-being, however rare and old they may be. Remembering the good times reminds you that a better life is possible and instills hope that it can be attained. Each story also recognizes that there are future chapters to come, and that you have the choice to make them play out as you wish.

Quite often, participants in the Bridges To Life program have never before told their story, particularly not to a group of empathetic listeners. Consider Robert. He was born in Fort Worth and adopted, along with an older sister, by a well-to-do older couple. Robert was hyperactive and regularly caused problems for his adoptive parents. They beat him and abused him emotionally and psychologically from an early age. Robert began running away from home when he was twelve. When his adoptive parents gave up on him, he was shuffled from foster home to foster home, institution to institution, from occasional love to continuing abuse, from freedom to incarceration. When not institutionalized, he supported himself by selling marijuana, cocaine, and other drugs; stealing; and doing favors for many of life's losers. He has been jailed too many times to remember and has been confined in state prison on several occasions. Not surprisingly, he has never thought deeply about who he is or why he has done what he has done. He has always needed to show off his manhood and has never had a safe opportunity to share his fears and vulnerabilities. Most importantly, others have never listened to him without hating, judging, or condemning. Just opening himself up—warts and all— in a safe environment where people really listen was perhaps the most empowering event of his life. Someone to listen made the difference.

Stories, the telling and the listening, are the foundation for empathy. Empathy means having insights into another person's thoughts and sharing feelings without needing to change them, walking a mile in the other's sandals, and seeing things from their point of view. When you put yourself in another person's shoes, you are likely to make a connection. Seeing things from another's perspective helps you avoid your own blinders, and when others sense your empathy, they become less fearful about revealing themselves to you. That is the magic of telling your stories and listening to other stories in the Bridges To Life experience.

OTHER WAYS TO TELL YOUR STORY

A Bridges To Life small group is not the only way you can tell your story and benefit from it. You may not be able to join an organized program, but you can tell your story in other ways in an effort to learn more about yourself and your situation. Two excellent ways of doing so are to engage in dialogue with a person you trust or to write in a journal—or both.

Dialogue

Dialogue is a conversation in which two or more people exchange information, ideas, opinions, or feelings. The purpose of dialogue is not to persuade someone to do something or win an argument, but rather to explore complex concerns, gain new insights and understandings, learn more about yourself or another person, or enjoy one another's company. In dialogue, people suspend their assumptions and beliefs in a free exploration of all things they want to talk about. Dialogue occurs when Bridges To Life participants tell their stories in small groups. Schoolmates talking at lunch or friends drinking coffee together at a local café are typically engaging in dialogue; as are families lingering around the dinner table; a young person talking quietly with a favorite parent, uncle, aunt, or grandparent; or people who have hurt one another just talking about themselves and listening to one another.

Dialogue is sometimes difficult because it requires two people to work together. People may be separated by miles, or one may be locked up in jail or prison, or they may refuse to engage in dialogue because they're afraid to expose their vulnerabilities.

You can, however, nearly always engage in dialogue if you want to. There are typically opportunities for conversation with family and friends: at meals, family gatherings, special events, home visits. You can ask your probation officer, a social worker, or a favorite schoolteacher, friend, or relative to talk quietly and confidentially. If you do not have a relationship with a person you would like to connect with—like an absentee father—you can swallow your pride and give that person a call. The response may be surprising. You can arrange to visit with a stranger whom you have hurt or who has hurt you.

The important point to remember is that the purpose of the communication is to exchange thoughts and ideas, not to solve problems, negotiate, persuade, or decide. You can get the dialogue going by asking the other person questions. Start with simple questions and gradually move to questions that are more important to your concerns. Encourage her to respond by listening carefully to what she is saying. Questions like these are likely to motivate her to ask you similar questions and allow you to begin telling your own story. If not, you can always respond to her answers with some of your own story.

Dialogue allows you and another person or persons to come to see each other differently, often by recognizing that you are more alike than you ever realized. It allows you to acknowledge each other as fellow human beings, with frailties, emotional pains, strengths, and potentials. Importantly, talking about yourself helps you build strength of self and identify who you really are, and listening to another person helps you to understand her point of view and empathize with her. The private, non-threatening opportunity to explain and humanize yourselves helps everyone involved discover that you can feel and express some degree of understanding and concern for one another even if you have a lot of disagreement.

The telling and the listening allows you to learn and think together; changes everyone involved; helps you become less fearful, defensive, and self-centered; and sets the stage for other efforts that will more directly address your concerns and problems.

Writing in Your Journal

Dialogue is an excellent process for learning: for you to learn about another person, for him to learn about you, and for each of you to learn more about yourself. However, when dialogue is not practicable, or when you want to concentrate on yourself, writing in a journal is an excellent thing to do.

A journal is a notebook in which you write about yourself, events of your life, what has happened to you, things you've done, your feelings, ideas, hopes, dreams. It is a day-to-day account in which you tell your story to yourself.

Writing in your journal can be a form of worship that brings God into your life, as you use your writing to record your thoughts, thanks, fears, and hopes while at the same time asking for God's help. A journal can also help you through an emotionally painful experience. Writing about pain focuses attention, acknowledges the pain, and avoids denial. Simply making lists of all the good things in life can help you deal with the bad things.

All you need to keep a journal is paper (preferably some type of notebook you can keep organized), a pen, and a few minutes each day to record what is important at the time. You can select topics and write all you can think about on certain ones. You can write lists of events in your life over a period of time. Or you can step back and describe in vivid detail your personal feelings, reactions, and points of view. Most who keep a journal combine these and other techniques to write what is helpful and meaningful to them at the current time.

Another idea, one used in Bridges To Life, is the unsent letter. Toward the end of the Bridges To Life experience, each participant is required to write two letters: one to a member of his family and the other to a victim of his crime. The letters to victims are not to be sent, and those to family members are not written to be sent, although they often are upon later reflection. The purpose and value is in the writing, not in the sending.

You can write such letters time and again. Writing an unsent letter is a powerful way of addressing your emotions about or toward another person. Doing so allows you to express your inner feelings as if you were face to face talking to him or her, without the person really having to be there. The letter helps you think about your emotions and the other person, and writing rids you of a lot of emotional baggage.

In summary, journal writing is a remarkable process for discovering and bringing to the surface what you already know. Journals serve many purposes. They can simply tell the story of events or chronicle happy times. They can also prepare you to confront those you've hurt or who have hurt you and resolve the issues between you. Writing about your life, like telling your story to someone else, creates a more complete picture of the parts of your life that are in your mind. The writing usually provides a discipline to your thinking that helps develop insights and solve problems. At a minimum, a journal is a safe way of blowing off steam, easing worry and obsession, and identifying your hopes and fears.

STUDY QUESTIONS

1. How does sharing of stories help us see our common humanity?
2. Why is it important for others to listen while we are telling our story?
3. How does listening to another person's story help you develop empathy for others?
4. Why was telling her story such an important step in Connie Hilton's healing process?
5. Why is honestly telling our story so difficult for many of us?
6. Why is your family such an important part of your story?

6

RESPONSIBILITY

"I can now understand there is a chain reaction that starts with me."
Inmate, Dominguez Unit

Responsibility is about cause and effect, and involves behavior and its consequences. Cause is the reason something happens. Effect—also called consequence—is the result. If a person is a cause of conflict, hurt, or a problem, he is responsible for it. Deciding who is responsible or what consequences they are responsible for often isn't easy, however. Many situations involve a number of actions and interactions that make assigning responsibility confusing.

The story of David, Bathsheba, and David's family from 2 Samuel 11-13 is a good example. David was king of Israel. He was an effective leader who used his great military power to bring peace to his nation, but his personal life was in shambles. He had a wandering eye and liked what he saw in Bathsheba, so he sought her out and committed adultery with her. He then tried to cover-up the adultery by having her husband, Uriah, assigned to the front lines of battle, where he was killed as expected. With her husband out of the way, David married Bathsheba, and they had a son, but the Lord made the son deathly sick and killed him as punishment for David's sin. Amnon, David's first-born son (by another wife) fell madly in love with Tamar (his half-sister, David's daughter by still another wife) and conspired with his cousin, Jonadab, to get her into bed. When his plan didn't work, he raped her and threw her out, destroying her chances of marrying because she was no longer a virgin. This greatly angered Absalom, Tamar's brother and another of David's sons, so he had his men get Amnon drunk and kill him. Absalom then incited a rebellion against David, and on and on.

What a mess! Who was responsible for what? Was David responsible for Tamar's rape because of the example he set for Amnon and the way he raised his son? Was Bathsheba responsible for her own adultery, even though it was with the powerful king of Israel? What responsibility, if any, did Bathsheba hold for the death of her son? Was Amnon responsible for his own murder because he raped Tamar, or was Absalom solely responsible? Was David responsible for the entire chain of events in his family? If so, does this mean Amnon and Absalom were not responsible for their own actions?

Does this biblical story remind you in any way of your family? Bridges To Life participants are often involved in similarly confusing situations. Richard's case is a good example. He is a twenty-seven year-old at the Le Blanc prison in Beaumont. He is five feet eight inches tall, a little chubby, broad in the beam, with a round, open, freckled face, big, saucer eyes, and an easy smile. His father, an alcoholic and drug addict, abused his mother, both emotionally and physically. Richard was a slow learner and did poorly in school. When he didn't meet his father's expectations, his father usually beat him severely with a razor strap or an especially designed paddle and locked him in his room for hours. His mother stood by, afraid to intervene. At an early age, Richard began to skip school, then run away from home for extensive periods of time. He dropped out of school during tenth grade, served a term in a juvenile detention facility, and then held a series of dead-end jobs, none of which would support his alcohol and drug habit. He began selling drugs and shoplifting to support himself and then moved on to burglary. He badly abused his live-in girlfriend, with whom he had one child, until she escaped. He is now serving his third prison term.

Who is responsible for Richard's alcohol and drug use, his abusive treatment of his girlfriend, his selling drugs, his burglaries? Is his father responsible because Richard's behavior is the predictable consequence of the way father treated son? Is his mother responsible because she refused to leave the abusive relationship and take Richard with her? Is the school system responsible because it didn't address his learning differences? Is the juvenile justice system responsible because it didn't fix him? Isn't Richard responsible for his own life?

Mavis' case presents the other side of the coin. She is an attractive twenty-eight-year-old blond mother of three, with eighteen months remaining on her sentence in the Henley unit. She has a history of drug violations and is incarcerated for forging checks. She is wracked with guilt and shame over the death of her second child at the age of nine months. The two were sleeping in the same bed, and when Mavis awoke, her child was dead. Although an autopsy showed the baby died of sudden infant death syndrome, Mavis's abusive husband convinced her it was her fault. He told Mavis that if she hadn't gone to sleep, the baby would still be alive. Mavis is filled with pain and remorse because she went to sleep! Is she really responsible for her child's death?

Answering such questions and deciding who is responsible for what in confusing situations requires a discussion of cause and effect. We often think of cause and effect (or consequence) as a very simple process, where x causes y, which in turn causes z, and so on. But life is not so simple, and cause-effect relationships are usually messy, circular, and often not at all clear. This can be true for any of four different reasons.

- It is often difficult to tell which action or event is a cause and which is a consequence, or whether an action is both a cause and an effect: the classic question of whether the chicken or the egg came first. Cause-effect frequently moves in circles, and whether you see an action as a cause or effect depends on where you start. For example, in the story of David and Bathsheba, was David a lecherous old man whose basic instincts caused him to see Bathsheba as desirable, or was she so desirable that she caused the instincts in David? Did Richard's father beat him because he did badly in school, or did Richard do badly in school because his father beat him?

- Actions always have several consequences, and any consequence usually has several causes. You may do just one thing, but your actions have effects in many different places. Actions are like throwing a stone into a still, silent pond—the stone hits the water in one place, but its effects move out in a circle and affect the surface of the water in many places. Thus, your actions usually have several effects, some perhaps obvious and intended, and others less significant or unintended. What is of little significance from your perspective may be an important effect from another's perspective. For example, think of all the effects of David's adultery with Bathsheba. He hurt her, Uriah died, David and Bathsheba's son died—all direct effects of David's actions. David's influence no doubt was a cause contributing to his son, Amnon, raping Tamar. Thus, David's act probably was a cause that helped destroy Tamar, made Absalom a murderer, and led to a rebellion against David. So many dire consequences from one impulsive act!

- Effects do not always follow causes closely in time or space. Some causes are direct and easy to see, while others are underlying, more basic, and often hidden from view. Consequences are often delayed and appear in different and unexpected areas. If we look for effects that are close in time and space we can often find apparent ones, but they may not be the only ones. Think again of David and Bathsheba. Their adultery was a clear, direct cause of their son's death, because the Lord took him as punishment for their actions. But Absalom's murder of Amnon was separated in time and space from the adulterous activity, even though David's murderous dishonesty and abuse of power probably influenced both of his sons and led to their destruction. Or think of Richard. Richard was directly responsible for his crimes because he did them. Richard's father was also responsible—although more remotely in time and space—because of his influence on Richard.

- The effect of an action is not always equal in size to the act itself. Sometimes actions get no reactions at all. Sometimes, large, seemingly important actions cause consequences that are much smaller than expected; while other times, small, apparently minor acts cause reactions that are much larger than expected. For example, Richard's mother did almost nothing. But her standing by and allowing his father to beat him no doubt had a major effect on Richard's future life.

In summary, our actions nearly always have many causes and many effects. Many influences cause us to do what we do, and our actions cause many consequences, some we can see and others we cannot see, and typically affect many people. And consequences are often bigger than we think they should be. The sale and use of alcohol and drugs is probably the best example of behavior that many claim has few or no bad consequences, but in fact hurts many people in many different ways.

Consider the life of Kimberly Buirst. Today Kimberly is a thirty-one year old single mom and Bridges To Life volunteer who is pursuing a degree in Criminal Justice at the Austin Community College. But in many respects her life has been a nightmare, not because of murder or assault or burglary or other things with obvious and immediate bad effects on her life. Instead, the drug dealers who contributed to her mom's abuse of alcohol and drugs have caused a lifetime of hurt for Kimberly and her sisters. Kimberly tells of being moved back and forth between her mother and her father and her father's ex-wife and her boyfriend, of—at age 13 and even after she had her own children—having to be a mother to her younger sister, of being molested by her mom's boyfriends and then always feeling dirty around men, of beginning to drink at age fifteen, of struggling in school, of marrying the first man who said he loved her and then divorcing, of the continuing shame of her mother now being incarcerated for selling drugs to an undercover agent. Kimberly has captured the continuing hurt from the actions of the drug dealers who sold to her mother, and from her mother's abuse, in the following poem:

Dear "Mr. Dope Man"

Dear "Mr. Dope Man," you must have sold your drugs to
    my momma.
She was just home this morning, but now we can't find
    her.

She's about five feet nine; she's a wife and mother.
Has three beautiful daughters and she's a grandmother.

Do you remember my mother? She helped you purchase
    those rims.
She took from the household for your drugs, now you
    marching around in "Tim's."

You know. That is a lot of ice gleaming from your mouth.
Was it all them double-ups that brought you so much
    clout?

I love my momma; I just don't understand her addiction;
You don't understand it either, you just on a money
    mission.

What if my shoes were on your feet and drugs had your
    mom turned out?
What if I took her parole dues and food from her family's
    mouth?

Has your mother ever ignored you while she was standing
    on a corner?
How could she give birth to a child and act like she don't
    know her?

I guess all that matters to you is fulfilling the dream.
Though selling that crack rock can't be all that it seems.

When she comes off her high, she's so filled with guilt.
Wanting hugs and kisses in the midst of this filth.

Dear "Mr. Dope Man," you've created a monster.
You've turned one of God's creations into a dope man's
    dumpster.

She was killing herself fast enough without any help from
    you.
Alcohol and suicide attempts now this drug abuse.

I know that you can hear me but if you are listening, take a
    stand.
Find something worth working for and retire from being
    the "Dope Man."

So much hurt—from the Dope Man who doesn't concede that he is responsible for it. This leads to the question of how, in this messy world, to sort out who is responsible for what, and more importantly, what we are responsible for.

ACCEPTING RESPONSIBILITY

Sometimes honestly assessing our responsibility in a matter immediately frees us from anxiety, because we see that we did not cause certain bad things that have been worrying us. At other times, however, thinking deeply about our responsibility creates a healthy guilt that leads to genuine remorse and healing. Healthy guilt helps us see and acknowledge the darker parts of our lives and accept the pain we are feeling. Guilt also prepares us to overcome our pain while at the same time avoiding hurtful shame over things that are not our fault or even our business. Therefore, assessing and accepting responsibility helps us define who we really are, identify what we need to change, and overcome the influences that are holding us where we are. Being responsible helps us develop a vision of where we need to be and the motivation to move in that direction.

How do you assess your own responsibility for what you have done, for where you are in life, and for the problems your family and friends are dealing with? Do you blame parents, relatives, or friends for your own actions? Do they blame you for theirs? Do you understand the consequences of your own behavior? From a different perspective, are you overcome by shame and guilt about something you shouldn't be blamed for? Your approach to answering such questions may be unhealthy or healthy.

Unhealthy Approaches to Responsibility

It's easy for us to avoid taking responsibility for our behavior. We often do so by denying that our actions were the cause of a particular situation, rationalizing away their consequences, or blaming others.

- Denial is when we hide from ourselves, repress our actions in our unconscious, pretend things didn't happen, or convince ourselves that consequences did not result. Denial means we don't see ourselves as we really are. For example, Richard's father may have blocked out his actions and simply denied that he used a razor strap on Richard. Or Richard may have blocked out the fact that his quitting school was the start of his downfall.

- Rationalization is where we allow our mind to construct false explanations or minimize the consequences of our actions. Using the same example, Richard's father is rationalizing when he acknowledges he used the strap to beat Richard but maintains that Richard needed it and the beating did him good. Richard rationalizes dropping out of school by pretending he had to in order to work.

- Blame is when we try to shift responsibility to someone else. We see our bad behavior as someone else's fault. When Richard blames his father for his own drug abuse and prison time, he is trying to avoid personal responsibility by blaming another person.

If we deny that our actions are a cause of a particular consequence, rationalize the consequences away, or unfairly blame another, we are not facing up to our responsibility.

On the other hand, feeling responsible about something that isn't our fault (like Mavis did) involves an unhealthy shame that has nothing to do with our behavior or its consequences. Instead, such false responsibility demonstrates our rejection of our worth as a human being. When we feel responsible for a happening that's outside our control, that event is likely to become part of who we are rather than simply how we view certain events in our life.

Offenders in the Bridges To Life program often have been masters of mishandling responsibility, and they provide excellent examples of how it happens. Alex, for example, claimed that he did not commit murder and that shooting a woman in the head was an accident, even though a jury said he murdered her. Sometimes juries are wrong, but often people deny the truth, as Alex did. Sally convinced herself that her addiction hurt only herself and that her drug sales were justified by her need for money. She was rationalizing. Jed said that he drove while drunk because his father was a drunk who frequently beat him. Jed was blaming. Recall Mavis, who felt responsible for the crib death of her child. She had an unhealthy guilt, resulting from feeling responsible when she wasn't.

Do you ever engage in denial, rationalization, or blaming? Do you ever feel an unjustified shame? The following section will offer thoughts on how you can better understand and accept responsibility for your own behavior.

Healthy Approaches to Responsibility

Why bother thinking about and accepting responsibility for conflicts and problems anyway? Isn't accepting responsibility just a form of "Monday morning quarterbacking" that allows others to criticize, blame, or pass the buck and leads to our feeling guilty? Isn't any problem we are dealing with a matter of the present rather than the past? Doesn't considering responsibility just cause us to hope for a better past that really isn't there? How does deciding who caused a problem help to build a more positive present or future? Shouldn't we just forget the past and move on to a better future?

Certainly, the past is over, and we cannot change what we or others have done. But understanding our past actions and their consequences—understanding and accepting our responsibility—is necessary for us to deal with what has happened and move to the future.

From one viewpoint, assigning responsibility might not be considered important, because every person should work to cure hurt and mend relationships regardless of who caused the problems. From another perspective, however, identifying responsibility tells us where the core of a problem is and puts an additional burden on the person or persons who caused it. If we don't respect another person's reality, or our anger gets out of hand, or we are a substance abuser, or we confuse respect with fear or envy, or we violate a law or other expectation, then we may be responsible for a problem. If we are, we need to take the lead in addressing it.

Accepting responsibility means acknowledging our own actions and the consequences that result from them. If we want to change as a person, we have to change our behavior: we have to change what we say and do, and not just how we think or feel. Accepting responsibility means that we acknowledge what we said or did and our role in the consequences. Accepting responsibility doesn't mean hoping for a better past. It means learning from history, so we can prevent bad history from repeating itself.

Accepting responsibility is necessary for healing one's self and one's relationship with others. It is necessary for the remaining steps in the Bridges To Life process for changing lives and relationships to work. You can't be accountable, confess, repent, or grant or seek forgiveness unless you identify what you should account for, confess to, and repent of, and who needs to forgive whom for what. Accepting responsibility is only the first step of a healing journey, but it's an absolutely essential first step.

The question is, how does one determine her own responsibility in a hurtful, conflict ridden situation. Sometimes who caused hurtful actions or failed relationships is not clear, and often people deny their roles in them or rationalize away the consequences or try to shift the blame.

If you have hurt someone, caused problems, or violated the law, you no doubt know who did what to whom, what you have done wrong, or how you have hurt others. But you may be like Richard, in the story introduced above. He acknowledged he committed burglary, violated a law, and hurt the one he burglarized. He admitted it in a plea bargain agreement. However, he continues to maintain "they had so much money they didn't really miss it." Further, he blames his dysfunctional parents for his own behavior and refuses to accept that he contributed to all the other consequences of his actions: the higher insurance rates, increased taxes for more policemen, fearful people, drug addiction, and other negative effects of his life that he is unable or unwilling to see. You may be in a similar situation, where you acknowledge you did something wrong, but put all the blame on someone else and refuse to acknowledge all the consequences of your action.

Notice that the conversation here concerns "a cause" and not "the cause," recognizing that there can be several causes of any problem, and that you bear responsibility if you were one of them. Think about Richard's story. Who caused his pattern of burglary? At first we feel anger and resentment toward only him. But as we think about his learning problems, the abuse in his family, his alcoholic father, his father's abuse of him, and his lack of support from his mother, the question becomes more difficult. But how far can we take this logic? Was Richard's behavior all a question of bad parenting, societal neglect, and social conditioning or is he also a cause of his behavior? Who ultimately is responsible? Richard? His father? His mother? A deficient school system? A justice system that did not rehabilitate him? All of the above? And did Richard, along with others, cause more problems and hurt than he is serving time for, such as the fear, anxiety, and broken lives of unseen victims of his drug dealing and other bad actions?

Richard's case is a little like a river. Several upstream causes came together to influence Richard to behave as he did, and his behavior caused downstream consequences to several people in addition to the specific victims. You may face similar situations in which you reacted to a number of influences, and you are one of several who had some influence on a problem and therefore are part of its cause.

When several people are the cause of some action and the action has several consequences, how do you determine your own responsibility? Two approaches can be helpful in deciding.

First, you can get a good idea about who is responsible by asking a series of "why" questions. "Why" questions help you look at both direct and indirect causes of hurt or broken relationships and determine who committed acts that caused, or at least contributed to, a problem. Why did someone get hurt? Why did certain things happen as a result of certain actions? Am I the one who did those things? Why did I do what I did? Asking such questions will help you discover all the causes of a situation, and help you identify your role, correct your behavior, and prevent similar situations from occurring in the future.

Using "why" questions to determine who or what caused a situation involves identifying the troubling event and then looking back in time by asking and honestly answering a series of questions, such as:

- Why is Richard in prison? Because he committed burglary.
- Why did Richard commit burglary? Perhaps because he needed money.
- Why did he need money? Perhaps because he couldn't hold a job.
- Why couldn't he hold a job? Perhaps because he was poorly qualified and addicted to drugs.
- Why was he poorly qualified? Perhaps because the school system let him down.
- Why was he addicted to drugs? Perhaps because his father was addicted and abused him.

- Why was his father able to abuse him? Perhaps because his mother allowed him to.

Thus, asking a series of "why" questions helps you look beneath the obvious and see who or what contributed to an event or its consequence. "Why" questions suggest in this case that several people were responsible. Richard was the direct cause of his imprisonment (and was responsible), because he is the one who committed the burglary. His father, mother, and the school system also contributed (and were also responsible). If you are involved in a problem, honestly ask yourself a series of "why" questions? Are you the answer to any of the questions? If so, you are at least a part of the cause, and you are responsible for the situation.

A second approach is to ask yourself a series of "if only" questions and honestly answer them. Ask yourself "If only I had (done or not done something), would the consequence have happened?" The key to success in this exercise is honesty. Dishonestly harping on "if only" questions can lead to unjustified and inappropriate shame while honestly answering them will lead either to freedom from or acknowledgment of responsibility.

Think of Mavis, whose daughter died of crib death while sleeping in the bed with her. Mavis can think of a million "if only" questions, and if she answers them honestly she must conclude that none of the actions would have prevented her daughter's death. If only she hadn't gone to sleep, would her child still be alive? Of course not. Mavis simply wasn't responsible, because doing anything differently would not have made a difference.

Now think of Richard, and the "if only" questions that could have been asked in his situation. For example:

- If only Richard's father had not abused him, and instead had been a good father, would Richard be in prison? Possibly not, so the father probably holds some responsibility.
- If only Richard had not committed burglary, would he be in prison? Probably not, so Richard is responsible for being in prison.

And on and on.

Accepting responsibility is the starting point. If we are responsible for a situation or problem, then we have to consider who we should answer to. That is the subject of the following chapter.

STUDY QUESTIONS

1. Describe an incident when you tried to avoid responsibility by denying what happened. By rationalizing what happened. By blaming someone else.
2. Think about the story of David, Bathsheba, and David's family. What do you think were some causes and effects of the actions of several of those biblical people?
3. What was the biggest conflict within your family when you were growing up? What caused it? What were its effects?
4. What is a time when you were responsible for a conflict or for someone being hurt?
5. Why did you do what you did that is causing you problems?
6. Who else contributed to your doing this?
7. Were you responsible for what you did?
8. What are some good things that have happened in your life? Who was responsible for them?

7

ACCOUNTABILITY

"It gave me the chance to open up and let my heart speak to the victims on a personal basis."
Inmate, Central Unit

L et's continue the story of David, Bathsheba, and David's family, introduced in Chapter 6. David committed adultery with Bathsheba, had her husband murdered, and raised sons who committed rape and murder and rebelled against the family. The story continues in Psalm 51, where David admits his shameful deeds and acknowledges that although Bathsheba, her husband, and his family were his direct victims, he has also sinned against God. He has hurt others but must answer to God because he has rebelled against His laws and ways of living. Because David is accountable to God, he admits his sins to Him, accepts his punishment, asks for forgiveness, and offers penance.

Or think again about Richard's story, also from Chapter 6. He felt that his addiction was hurting only himself and his burglary was against unknown, unnamed victims. He was required to answer to society and the state because he broke society's laws and was responsible for his behavior. That's why he is in prison. Richard no doubt should have been answerable to others as well: perhaps his parents who in some weird way loved him, even though they abused him, perhaps some friends, certainly himself.

Both David and Richard were responsible for crimes against other people, and both were answerable—accountable—for their actions. What does this mean, and how can people deal with their need to be accountable? Answering such questions is the topic of this chapter.

ABOUT ACCOUNTABILITY

Accountability means being answerable and implies a legal, moral, or other obligation to someone as though he is sitting in judgment and can in some way call you to account. You are accountable to someone when you have a duty to him or her. While responsibility is largely a matter of your own behavior and who you are, accountability is based on rules, expectations, or judgments by yourself and others about whether your actions are praiseworthy or blameworthy and who you are answerable to.

Accountability may arise from a formal relationship, such as our obligations under the law or by specific, written contract. For example, we are answerable to the state to obey its laws and to a creditor to repay a loan. More often, however, accountability is informal, based on relationships and unstated expectations of those you care about or love and those who care about or love you. You are being accountable when you accept responsibility for your actions and recognize your obligation to make things right with those who have a legitimate expectation of you. Thus, being accountable is mainly a state of mind that recognizes the valid need, expectation, or right of another person. It's always there, but becomes particularly relevant when one accepts responsibility for his behavior and plans to answer for what he has done by taking healing actions such as those discussed in the remainder of this book.

Think about problems, broken relationships, or crimes that you are dealing with. Who is responsible for them, and what does accountability mean for you? What are you accountable for and to whom? Who is accountable to you?

You are accountable if you are responsible, your actions were inappropriate, you had a choice, and you have a duty to someone. Each of these aspects of accountability will be discussed below.

You Are Responsible

Accountability flows from responsibility. A person is not accountable if he is not responsible, but is likely to be accountable if he is responsible: if he caused a conflict, a problem, or a crime. You are generally accountable for what you are responsible for (some exceptions are discussed below), and others are accountable for what they are responsible for. Thus, several people may be accountable in any situation if their actions helped cause it. Richard, for example, answered to the state and went to prison because he was responsible for the burglaries he committed. His parents, who did not go to prison for their contribution to their son's behavior, are nevertheless accountable (to someone—see below) because they also were at least partially responsible for his actions. If the school system also contributed to the problem, it may also be accountable.

Your Actions Were Inappropriate

If you caused a problem, hurt someone, or violated the law, then your behavior was probably inappropriate. You probably did what you should not have done rather than what you ought to have done.

Sometimes, however, you can do the right thing and still cause problems. For example, assume you have a friend who committed a burglary, you observed the burglary, and you turned him in to the law; and as a result his family, formerly close friends, will not speak to you. You were legally and morally required to turn him in, yet your actions caused the problem. If you hadn't turned him in, you and the burglar's family would still be friends. Your right and appropriate action has caused a problem. But are you morally accountable for the consequences if you did the right thing? No, some things need to be done, regardless of the consequences. In a case where you did nothing wrong you may wish to take the initiative to mend your relationship, but not because you are answerable for a wrong.

When you commit a crime, you do something wrong and you are accountable for your actions. Sometimes, however, you do things and you are not sure whether they are right or wrong. For example, you cover for a friend who is lying, skip school or work without a really good reason, or assault someone who insulted your sister even though she wasn't hurt and you could have left the scene.

Thinking about the following questions will help you assess your actions and decide whether they were appropriate or inappropriate.

- How do you feel about what you did? Most people have a pretty good understanding of right and wrong, good and bad, and you probably do as well. You know whether your actions show love, kindness, generosity, truth, or justice; or whether they show hatred, self-interest, one-upmanship, or exploitation of someone without power or a voice. Just as you know the color blue when you see it, you usually know right and wrong, good or bad when you see them.

- Were your actions consistent with the teachings of your religious tradition? In Chapter 4 we briefly discussed the teachings of Christianity as a great moral code, emphasizing the Ten Commandments, the Sermon on the Mount, and the Golden Rule as examples. The Ten Commandments require that we honor our father and mother, and they prohibit worshipping other gods or idols, murder, adultery, stealing, lying, and envy. The Sermon on the Mount asks us to look at our motives and our heart. The Golden Rule—to do to others only that which you would wish them to do to you— provides good direction. These or other principles of your religious tradition are guideposts that provide a blueprint for living and help you distinguish right from wrong, good from bad.

- Did your actions aim to do the most good for the greatest number? This question has you focus on the likely consequences of your actions. While you cannot always predict with certainty what the consequences will be, you have a feel for the answers. Like understanding what is right and wrong, most people can understand the consequences of most of their actions if they are honest with themselves. Thus, honestly considering the consequences will provide important guidance in assessing your own behavior.

- Did your actions or inaction violate a rule or law? Rules and laws are generally established to protect a larger group or society at large from the acts of an individual. Therefore, while you may believe that a violation will benefit you, unless there are special and unique circumstances, your illegal act is likely to harm the larger group. Thus, if you are violating a rule or law, your actions are almost surely inappropriate.

If you feel what you did was right, your behavior was consistent with your religion, what you did caused the greatest happiness to the greatest number, and you did not violate any rule or law, then you probably are not accountable for the consequences even though you may have been a cause of some hurt. However, if you ask these questions about your behavior and get different answers, you probably are accountable to someone for the consequences of your actions.

You Had a Choice in the Matter

In rare cases you may not be accountable for your actions, even if you are responsible and they were inappropriate. Notions of accountability, blame-worthiness, and praise-worthiness for actions are related to notions of free will: to questions of whether our actions are inevitable and not determined by us or whether we have choices about our actions.

Most people agree that our desires and our whole character are greatly influenced by the lessons and experiences of our childhood. However, most people—and certainly the law and justice systems—do not believe that such external factors require us to do what we do or prevent us from doing what we ought to do. They believe we have freedom of choice.

We lose our freedom of choice only when we are actually prevented from doing something or compelled to do something by something outside our control. A person's actions are not free, for example, if he is not physically capable of doing something, or has been drugged by someone else, unreasonably threatened, or placed under hypnotic suggestion. We are free when we do not act under compulsion and are able to choose our own course of action or act according to our own choices or desires. Thus, a person's actions are free if he, like Richard, had the final choice, even if experiences from earlier life made his choice more difficult than those many of us face.

An essential aspect of human beings as persons rather than animals is our ability to want to be different in our preferences and purposes than we are. Many animals have desires to do one thing or another. But only we human beings have the capacity to look internally at ourselves and make our own choices, even if our basic desires are determined by genes and environment. This basic difference—our ability to want to change and to change—sets us apart, gives us free will, and makes us responsible for our actions unless we are actually prevented by an external force from doing something or compelled to do something.

Some people, such as the insane, do not have to be accountable because they do not have a free will. But nearly all situations involve the opposite. Essentially all adults in our society have a free will nearly all the time. No doubt genes and the environment in which a person is raised affect his decisions and his actions—and perhaps even make them predictable. Such factors, however, do not take away a person's free will. Given Richard's dysfunctional, abusive family, one could reasonably predict he would go astray. But saying his behavior was predictable is not to say that he was being controlled or manipulated, or that he did not have free choice in matters of behavior. Since Richard was not under compulsion or restraint, he was accountable for his behavior. Others with similar histories have chosen different paths, and Richard could have done so as well. The choice was his.

You Have a Duty to Answer to Someone

Accountability arises from a social contract—sometimes agreed and written, but usually unstated and often unacknowledged—that you have with another person, government, or entity. Like it or not, Richard had a "contract" with the state to abide by its laws, and his parents had a "contract" with him to raise, love, and protect him. Such contracts set out what can reasonably be expected of you and the other person or persons in your relationship. They establish, perhaps informally, your rights and obligations: what each of you is responsible for doing and not doing, what you can expect from the other, and what the other should be able to expect from you. Accountability follows the expectation.

You are accountable to those who have reasonable expectations of you and to whom you owe an explanation, usually including yourself, your God, your parents, others with whom you have a relationship, and society at large. For example, you might have a duty to answer to the following:

- Yourself because of your own expectations
- Your God because of His law and your belief in it
- A business partner or boss because of a written legal contract
- Your parents because of their reasonable expectations of you
- A stranger because you want to do the right thing and the law provides him various protections
- To society at large because of society's expectations as expressed primarily through its legal system

Sometimes accepting that we have a duty to answer to a person is difficult, particularly when that person's actions seem to suggest she doesn't deserve an answer. Demarcus is a twenty-two year old inmate, serving a five year sentence in the Kyle unit for an aggravated assault—an assault that occurred when he was high on cocaine. He is six feet four inches tall, good looking, and has the muscular build of a person who hits the gym every day. Tears rolled down his face as he talked of his mother: "I didn't have a real mother. Sure, she gave birth to me. But she was never there for me when I was a kid. She was more interested in alcohol and drugs with her boyfriends. Then she was sent to prison, although things weren't all that much different with her locked away. I was moved from my auntie to my grandmother to a foster home. I'll never forget the time my grandfather gave me some new shoes for school, and my mother stole them and sold them for drug money. My mother caused me a lot of pain, and she didn't have to. I tried to keep the pain inside and just put her out of my mind. I was mad—but mostly sad. I didn't think about accountability when I was a kid, but no way did I owe her an answer for anything. She did wrong by me."

Demarcus was quiet for several long seconds as he wiped tears from his face. Then he continued, "One day—probably when I was about seventeen—I said some really mean things to her. I'll never forget the look on her face. I knew then that she really loved me. As I have thought about her over the last few years, I've realized that although she did me wrong, she tried to look out for me. She had her own problems. And she was my mother, who still loves me. And I now feel accountable to her. I have to answer to her as to why I'm locked up."

People are imperfect, and some are more imperfect than others. But that doesn't mean we are not accountable to them.

We have discussed accountability primarily from your viewpoint. But accountability cuts both ways. Where you have a relationship with another, that person is also accountable to you, based on your reasonable expectation of him and his duty to you. For example, Richard was accountable to many people, including his father, for his bad behavior, but his father was also accountable to him for the way he raised him. Accountability to one another is the glue that holds our relationships together, or the magnet that pulls people toward one another when relationships are broken and need to be restored.

DEALING WITH ACCOUNTABILITY

To summarize, we have seen from the previous section that you are accountable if you are fully or partially responsible for a conflict, problem, or crime; your actions were inappropriate; you had a choice in the matter; and you have a duty of answering to someone. Further, accountability cuts both ways, as you are accountable to others and others to you. I can think of no better teacher for dealing with accountability than Jan Brown, a Bridges To Life victim volunteer who has dealt effectively with accountability from both directions.

Jan grew up in a troubled home and was psychologically, physically, and sexually abused during her childhood. Although her father did not abuse her, his behavior convinced her that children were objects to control rather than people to love. She married at a young age and soon had two children, a controlling mother, a divorce, and an ex-husband to deal with. Jan candidly and remorsefully states that she was not as good a mother as she would like to have been; and although she did not abuse her two older children as much as she had been, she had a tendency to raise them a lot like she was raised.

When Jan learned that she was carrying her third child, she didn't want to be pregnant, didn't believe she could become pregnant, was told by doctors that she would not be able to carry the baby to term. But her life was never the same after Kandy was born. Kandy's birth, life, and death got Jan's attention and taught her so much about accountability.

Kandy seemed like a miracle baby from the very start. Jan felt the first time she saw Kandy that her new daughter was someone very special, as though they were two parts of the same person. Kandy had a spontaneous personality, self-assurance, and a spark that made her special to everyone with whom she came in contact—her parents, grandparents, friends, and strangers alike. Very soon Jan realized that she, the mother who had been raising Kandy's siblings, owed them more and needed to change. For the first time Jan felt accountable to her children for her "parenting behavior." Jan recalls, "I specifically remember the time that I realized I didn't have to say 'no' to everything my children asked for and recognized children were people too, and not objects of control and hate."

Kandy bloomed into a beautiful, active, fun nine-year-old and lived with her father and stepmother in Bryan, Texas. Although Jan lived in the Houston area, she saw her daughter often, and the two loved being together. They spent the weekend of May 9 together, shopping, eating, seeing a movie, doing things mothers and daughters do when they love one another.

Jan's former husband, Kandy's father, called on Tuesday evening, May 12. "Jan, Kandy is missing, and they suspect foul play."

"I'll be right there."

"No. You need to stay at home. They suspect she was trying to get to you and may have asked the person who took her to take her to you. If she calls, you need to be there."

Jan knew immediately that her world had "just changed in a way that will never be the same. You don't yet know how, and you don't know what."

What do you do? What do you say to grandparents, siblings, all those who love Kandy so much? And how do you get through the night? On Wednesday afternoon Jan, in her head, seemed to hear Kandy say "Mommy, I'm okay." At that point Jan knew the ultimate truth—she knew that Kandy was dead.

About two weeks later, what remained of Kandy's body was found in a wooded field when a local man out for a walk investigated the odor from her small, decaying body and saw her feet protruding from a pile of rubbish. A "350 pound, stinking junk dealer" had picked her up after school and eventually tied her hands behind her back and shot her point-blank in the face in her full view. Kandy's body was unrecognizable except for her feet, "worse than you could possibly imagine." Looking at the contents of that body bag was the most devastating part of Jan's long journey. Because of her experience, she is now helping offenders understand their own accountability.

What does this tragic story and its aftermath teach us about accountability? It teaches us that we should acknowledge our accountability for our own actions, and we often need to hold others accountable for their responsibilities. These two sides of the same coin will be discussed in the sections that follow.

Being Accountable

What is it like to acknowledge our accountability? What can we learn from Jan recognizing her accountability to her older children? Let's look at what she did. While faced with healing the tragedy in her own life, she came to realize she was accountable to her two older children and needed to heal her relationships with them. She acknowledged the terrible pain and emptiness caused by denying that she had mistreated them and recognized the need to tell them the truth about what she had done. Jan says, "The two most healing words in the English language are 'I'm sorry,' which I have said to each of them at least a million times and will continue to say for at least another million if necessary. For their well-being and mine, no subject is off-limits if they want to talk about it. I will be accountable for my actions for as long as I live."

To help put Jan's actions in context, let's look at the opposite, where someone never acknowledged responsibility or accepted accountability.

Chris Castillo is the youngest of three children, the only boy. Although his parents divorced when Chris was twelve, he grew up in a safe, loving home, primarily because of the influence of his mother, Pilar. Chris and his mother had a special relationship, even after he married and had his own child. They were mother and son, and also best friends. It was not uncommon for them to eat a meal and then sit talking so long that it was time for the next meal.

Chris was at work on his news reporting job in Beaumont on November 20 when he received that terrible call, "Your mother is dead." Chris drove to Houston, where his mother lived, completely befuddled about his mother's death at age fifty-two. What could have happened? He realized that something was terribly wrong when he turned on to her street and saw police cars and news reporters. Chris watched on television from his neighbor's house as they brought his mother's body from her home. Workers who had been renovating her house had murdered her. They woke her up during the night, forced her to sign blank checks, strangled her to death, and then put her back into bed.

Chris often tells his story to Bridges To Life groups. Each part is tragic and compelling, but none more than when he discusses the murderers' lack of accountability. They fled the country, to Honduras, and have never been caught. Their story is a real life example of how so many of us fail to acknowledge accountability for our actions: we run away mentally and emotionally, fail to recognize or face up to the needs of others, are unwilling to answer for what we have done.

The difference between Jan's answering to her children and the murderers of Chris' mother running away demonstrates what it takes to be accountable. Jan did not run away, either physically, mentally, or emotionally, but instead accepted that:

- She was responsible for her behavior in raising her children. Her actions had a direct effect on them.
- She had not behaved appropriately toward her children. When Kandy was born she realized that her negative approach was not the way she should parent and that she needed to begin the healing process.
- She had a choice in the matter. Her own parents had shown her the wrong way, but they had not taken away her ability to choose.
- She had a duty toward her children and an obligation to answer to them for her behavior.
- Her first obligation was to be accountable to herself.

When Jan accepted these five facts she, unlike the murderers who ran away, acknowledged her accountability. Doing so opened the door to actions that would improve her relationship with her children, and she has subsequently faced up to her situation and become the mother and grandmother that she knows she needs to be and that her children love.

Who are you answerable to? What behavior should you be accountable for? These are threshold questions. Once you have answered them, the remaining chapters of this book will offer suggestions for what to do to address your accountability.

Holding Others Accountable

Jan held herself accountable to her children, and she's among the best I've ever seen at holding others accountable as well. A good example occurred during a Bridges To Life session at the Walls unit in Huntsville when Jan held Lawrence accountable.

Lawrence grew up in a middle-class community in Houston. He had a better-than-okay childhood: loving parents, Boy Scouts, football, prom, graduation, trade school. He married at age twenty-two and supported his young family by working in a series of auto repair shops. At age thirty-one, Lawrence and his best high-school friend pooled their savings, borrowed heavily, and purchased a used car dealership. The business was a struggle but eventually began to do well.

Over a period of time Lawrence came to the conclusion that his partner was taking money from the till and decided to confront him. They agreed to go to a local park to talk in private. Heated words were exchanged, emotions escalated. Lawrence went to his truck, got his 22-caliber pistol, and killed his friend. Lawrence is now serving twenty-five years. On several occasions in small group meetings, Lawrence avoided discussing the murder by noting he was in prison because he "caught me a case."

Jan had enough. When Lawrence one more time talked about "catching a case," Jan responded with just the right combination of love, concern, and frustration. "Lawrence, don't try to feed me that b.s. You didn't catch a case. You got mad, went to your truck, got a gun, and murdered your best friend. You need to go to that man's mother and beg for forgiveness," she told him.

Lawrence's startled reaction showed Jan had gotten his attention, and he now understood accountability. Jan was able to hold him accountable because:

- She knew, from her own tragic experience, what Lawrence's victim's mother was feeling and was able to speak knowledgeably for her.
- She acted out of love for Lawrence and a desire to help him.
- She knew Lawrence could not get his life together unless he acknowledged his accountability for his actions.

Jan saw the truth when Lawrence could not, forced Lawrence to see the truth as well, and did so with love and concern. She demonstrated the essence of holding someone accountable. Similarly, if we love someone and are concerned about her, we need to hold her accountable for her actions.

STUDY QUESTIONS

1. Think about when you were responsible for hurting someone. How do you feel about what you did? What does your religious tradition say about what you did? Did your actions do good or bad for those involved? Did you violate the law? Are you accountable?
2. Did you have a choice about hurting the person?
3. Are you accountable for your actions today? If so, who are you accountable to or who do you need to come clean with?
4. Describe what it means to "be a real man" if you are male or to "be a real woman" if you are female.
5. Someone said, "sooner or later, you gotta come clean." What does this mean to you?
6. Do you have someone you can ask to hold you accountable for your actions? If so, list two or three people.

8

CONFESSION

"I am so sorry."
Inmate, Halbert Unit

The story of the Prodigal Son from Luke 15 demonstrates the healing power of confession and provides a basis for this chapter.

A man had two sons. When the younger told his father, "I want my share of your estate now, instead of waiting until you die!" his father agreed to divide his wealth between his sons.

A few days later this younger son packed all his belongings and took a trip to a distant land, and there wasted all his money on parties and prostitutes. About the time his money was gone a great famine swept over the land, and he began to starve. He persuaded a local farmer to hire him to feed his pigs. The boy became so hungry that even the pods he was feeding the swine looked good to him. And no one gave him anything.

When he finally came to his senses, he said to himself, "At home even the hired men have food enough and to spare, and here I am, dying of hunger! I will go home to my father and say, "Father, I have sinned against both heaven and you, and am no longer worthy of being called your son. Please take me on as a hired man.'"

So he returned home to his father. And while he was still a long distance away, his father saw him coming, and was filled with loving pity and ran and embraced him and kissed him.

His son said to him, "Father, I have sinned against heaven and you, and am not worthy of being called your son—."

But his father said to the slaves, "Quick! Bring the finest robe in the house and put it on him. And a jeweled ring for his finger; and shoes! And kill the calf we have in the fattening pen. We must celebrate with a feast, for this son of mine was dead and has returned to life. He was lost and is found." So the party began.

Confessing means admitting we have been wrong and acknowledging or disclosing our misdeeds, faults, or sins, just as the prodigal son did. We make a good, ol' fashioned apology. Confessing is the action that needs to follow from accepting responsibility and being accountable. It's a logical next step, the "proof of the pudding."

- First, we acknowledge that our acts cause certain consequences and therefore we are responsible.
- Second, we accept that we are accountable or answerable to someone.
- Third, we answer. Confession is the act we take when we are responsible and accountable and acknowledge both to someone.

When we insist we are right, we get awfully lonely. But when we admit we make mistakes and are flawed, we have lots of company. Admitting we are wrong confirms our honesty, our morality, and our strength, and allows us to reclaim our dignity. Confession helps us join the human race.

We can confess in any of four situations. Some people—often the case with Bridges To Life offenders—confess to law enforcement officials because they have violated a law and are accountable to the state and society. We confess to ourselves when we are intellectually honest about our faults and shortcomings. We confess to God when we acknowledge our sins and begin to restore relations with Him. We confess to another person as a way of telling her that we are strong enough to be accountable for our actions but also are a vulnerable human being who is willing to take the risks of laying out our shortcomings.

When we confess our mistakes to the state and fellow human beings, we begin to be a force for peace and reconciliation. When we acknowledge our shortcomings to ourselves, God, and man, we begin to be fully human and at peace with ourselves.

The Bridges To Life experience respects the importance of all four types of confession. All are discussed in the sections that follow.

CRIMINAL LAW CONFESSION

In criminal law, confession is a statement made by a person charged with the commission of a crime in which he acknowledges he is guilty of the offense charged and explains his role in it. The acknowledgment is to a law enforcement official and usually takes the place of a trial, which makes confession an important part of our country's criminal justice system.

Confessions to law enforcement officials are part of the prison background. Many offenders are incarcerated on the basis of their confession. Some get tired of running, allow themselves to be caught, and confess as a matter of course; while others resist to the end but ultimately confess as part of a plea bargain that avoids a trial or other judicial action. Others go to trial, lose their case, and subsequently confess. Regardless of how it happens, legal confession is something most offenders have experience with as part of their time in the criminal justice system. Therefore, this aspect of confession is not a significant point of discussion during the Bridges To Life experience.

CONFESSING TO YOURSELF

We also need to confess our faults and shortcomings to ourselves. As discussed in Chapter 6, people are often dishonest with themselves and use denial, rationalization, and blame to avoid facing up to what they have done and their responsibility for the consequences of their behavior. Quite a few Bridges To Life offenders seem to have confessed their crime to a law enforcement or other official without ever honestly and sincerely confessing to themselves. What they agreed (perhaps with some level of pressure) they had done, they still deny to themselves. However, when they confess to themselves—honestly admit their crimes, faults, and shortcomings—they are actually accepting responsibility and being accountable.

Confessing a misdeed to ourselves is our way of being honest in dealing with what we have done: avoiding denial, rationalization, and blame and clearly affirming that we have accepted responsibility and are accountable. Hiding from ourselves by pushing our behavior into the deep recesses of our unconscious or trying to explain it away keeps us broken, fearful, and at some level both arrogant and afraid of ourselves at the same time. It makes us dishonest, and therefore unable to deal honestly with others.

Clyde, a thirty-eight year-old inmate at the Kyle unit, is a good example. He owned his own house and had a generally stable family life, with two young children and a wife who loved him and a good relationship with his parents. He owned and operated a catering service that did a good business in the Houston area, particularly during holidays. But on the side, and without his family being aware of it, he ran a thriving drug business. He specialized in marijuana and cocaine but stayed away from heroin, claiming "that stuff is bad. It'll mess with you." He is now serving a five-year term for dealing drugs.

Clyde was unable to confess to himself at the beginning of the Bridges To Life experience. At some place in his mind he knew what he had done, but was able to separate the rest of his life, remembering his supportive family and catering business while largely denying his drug life. He seemed fearful of even talking about his actions, their consequences, or his accountability and was unable to deal honestly with himself. How could he deal honestly with others if he couldn't with himself? He couldn't. He had to start by confessing to himself.

Confessing to yourself is your journey to find truth, to quit lying to yourself about your behavior and its consequences, and to affirm that you really are responsible and accountable. You can use either or all of the following ways to confess to yourself:

- Prepare for prayer. The next section discusses confessing to God, and confessing to Him in prayer requires preparation. You cannot acknowledge or ask for something until you know what to acknowledge or ask for. Thus, you have to think about yourself and assess your own faults and needs before you pray. This preparation and prayer is one way of confessing to yourself.

- Write in your journal. Keeping a journal can be a form of confession in solitude, where you open your heart through writing about yourself. By writing in a journal you can confess secrets, emotions, pain, and shame that you do not yet feel you can share with anyone. You can surrender yourself with the certain knowledge that you will never be rejected, scolded, reprimanded, or betrayed. Since only you and God know what you are writing, you can know that you will be accepted and loved.

- Write a letter and don't send it. Unsent letters, a form of journal, can be very effective because thinking of a specific recipient and how you may have offended her helps you be more specific in your confession to yourself. The following excerpt from an unsent letter written by a Kyle inmate summarizes the value of confessing to yourself: "I have learned through bitter experience that if I intend to grow into emotional stability and to enter into the maturity of adulthood, I must look upon my many shortcomings with an open, understanding mind, see them for what they are, and take steps to correct them."

CONFESSING TO GOD

An honest relationship with God is impossible if we deny our faults and don't come clean with Him. The Bible teaches that we must confess our sins to be saved and to receive God's life within us. Confession practices vary widely, of course, from the more formal, confidential Sacrament of Penance in the Roman Catholic Church to less formal, sometimes more public confessions of other Christian traditions. It is a foundation of Christian teaching, however, that confession is necessary for a person to experience forgiveness.

To help us think in general terms about how we should confess to God, let's continue with the story of David, introduced in the discussion on responsibility in Chapter 6 and continued in Chapter 7. David was truly sorry for his adultery with Bathsheba, for murdering her husband to cover it up, and for his other sins. Psalm 51: 1-6 tells of his confession to God:

> O loving and kind God, have mercy. Have pity upon me and take away the awful stain of my transgressions. Oh, wash me, cleanse me from this guilt. Let me be pure again. For I admit my shameful deed—it haunts me day and night. It is against you and you alone I sinned, and did this terrible thing. You saw it all, and your sentence against me is just. But I was born a sinner, yes, from the moment my mother conceived me. You deserve honesty from the heart; yes, utter sincerity and truthfulness. Oh, give me this wisdom.

David reflected on his confession, and the joy of God's forgiveness for his sins against Bathsheba and Uriah, in Psalm 32: 3-5:

> There was a time when I wouldn't admit what a sinner I was. But my dishonesty made me miserable and filled my days with frustration. All day and all night your hand was heavy on me. My strength evaporated like water on a sunny day until I finally admitted all my sins to you and stopped trying to hide them. I said to myself, "I will confess them to the Lord." And you forgave me! All my guilt is gone.

We all need to confess to God in our own special way, according to the dictates of our own spiritual tradition. Using David as a model will be helpful. You can pray to God and confess what you've done.

CONFESSING TO OTHERS

Confessing guilt, inappropriate behavior, or sin to another person, particularly one you have hurt or sinned against, is the fourth type of confession. Doing so can have either or both of two different purposes. First, you can reveal something to someone you've hurt that the person doesn't already know. For example, you might have been cheating on your girlfriend or involved in a secret affair, and you need to admit your behavior to her. The telling is a form of confession.

Second, confession is a way of communicating that you are accepting responsibility and being accountable for actions that the other person is already aware of. This kind of confessing conveys your feelings or state of mind about what you have done. For example, assume you have treated your spouse badly and failed for years to meet his or her needs. Your spouse knows the situation, but you can still confess—you can acknowledge what you've done, the devastating consequences of your actions, and your willingness to answer for your behavior.

However, confessing to others doesn't always mean confessing to one we have hurt or have a relationship with. Part of the healing value of confession is being listened to, and a neutral person is often a better listener than someone who is directly involved. We often need someone to listen to our confession without any personal interest and without agreeing or disagreeing with us. Just telling our story to a good listener helps us see things as they really are and can be a dress rehearsal for our confession to someone we have hurt. Some of us have wise friends who are willing to listen and hold us accountable; while others may need to find a pastor, counselor, psychologist, or other appropriate professional.

Famed psychiatrist Dr. Carl Jung described the value of confession in the following quotation borrowed from *Problems in Modern Psychotherapy:*

> To cherish secrets and hold back emotion is a psychic misdemeanor for which nature finally visits us with sickness—that is when we do these things in private. But when they are done in communion with others they satisfy nature and may even count as useful virtues…. There would appear to be a conscience in mankind which severely punishes everyone who does not somehow and at sometime, at whatever cost to his virtuous pride, cease to defend and assert himself, and instead confess himself fallible and human. Until he can do this, an impenetrable wall shuts him off from the vital feeling that he is a man among other men. This explains the extraordinary significance of genuine, straightforward confession—a truth that was probably known to all the initiation rites and mystery cults of the ancient world. There is a saying from the Greek mysteries, "Give up what thou hast, and then thou wilt receive." [1]

We've talked about what confession does for us. Think now about what it does for the person we confess to. Confessing puts our offending behavior in the background and demonstrates our feelings and honesty. It shows us as we really are, and this honesty begins to build trust in the other person. When he hears us tell the difficult, shameful, risky truth, he is more likely to believe he can depend on us in the future.

Confession can begin a cycle of improvement in a relationship when one person responds to another person's behavior. Unfortunately, we often see negative actions met with negative actions, threats with threats, or silence with silence. The first action sets the tone, and unless one person or the other breaks the sequence, conflict grows to increasingly serious behavior. We can, however, also experience cycles of improvement, and confession is often the starting point. Most conflicts or problems involve some responsibility or fault on both sides, and when one person confesses, a repeating cycle begins. The door is open, and the other person responds to a confession by also confessing. When this happens, the people find their way to reconciliation and a better relationship.

Confessing one's inappropriate, hurtful actions to the one we have hurt is usually difficult and often takes real courage. Saying "I was wrong, and I am sorry" takes more guts than some of us have. Think of what was going through Danny's mind during a small group meeting at the Kyle unit. Danny is a handsome, clean-cut, wholesome twenty-four-year old former college student who had a very bright future—on the surface, every mother's dream—until he got drunk and killed two people in a car crash. Danny is now serving two twenty year sentences stacked, meaning he will serve a minimum of twenty and a maximum of forty years for his crime.

Kathy Connell (whose story is told in Chapter 12), a participant in the same small group, lost four children to another drunk. Think of Danny's feelings as he confesses to Kathy. He cannot really understand the pain Kathy suffers or how his confession may affect her, so he is afraid of what his confession will do to Kathy and afraid of how she will react. He is ashamed of his behavior, and his shame is made worse when he talks about what he has done. His pride also holds him back. He is proud of his accomplishments in many areas and doesn't want them diminished by confession of his major weakness, alcoholism. He wonders whether acknowledging his mistakes isn't a sign of weakness rather than a sign of strength. Denying responsibility for what happened, or trying to rationalize away the consequences, would be much easier.

You may have similar feelings about something you have done. Pride, fear, shame, or other concerns may be preventing you from confessing. You should get over these feelings, however, because confessing is essential to dealing effectively with your problems and relationships that need mending. You need to think seriously about when to confess, and how you should go about it.

When to Confess

Only you can decide when you need to confess an inappropriate action or misdeed. Before you do, however, be sure you can confess honestly and sincerely. A dishonest, insincere confession will do more harm than good: it will put you deeper in the hole of your own faults and shame. Rather than free you, it will entrap you. Rather than confirm your honesty, morality, and strength it will lead to a cycle of lying, immorality, and weakness. Rather than reclaim your dignity, it will speed your decline. You can fake it sometimes, for a short time, but not every time, or for long.

When you are dishonest or uncommitted, others will know. If they don't see the real you immediately, your future behavior will betray you. Those to whom you confessed dishonestly will become more cynical about you, less trusting of you. Ask Sonja and Dianeta and Marilyn and Dora and Jane and all the other abused woman who tell their stories during the Bridges To Life experience. Without fail, their abusers engaged in a cycle of abuse and lying masked as confessions: they abused and "confessed," abused and "confessed," and on and on. The abused women say that the physical abuse itself was only slightly more destructive of their relationship than the lying and hypocrisy involved in the dishonest confessions.

So what is an honest confession? An honest confession is possible when you are true to God, yourself, and others in genuinely accepting responsibility for what you have done, wishing to confess and acknowledge your accountability, and being committed to turn from your misdeeds and reform your life and your relationship with the other person.

Confessing requires looking both backward and forward. Look back to Chapter 6, where we saw that accepting responsibility means being honest about what you've done and its consequences, and to Chapter 7, which noted that being accountable means recognizing whom you need to answer to and starting with a confession. Look forward to Chapter 9, which discusses turning from your misdeeds and reforming your life, the essence of repentance.

You can confess to yourself and to God whenever the spirit moves you, but confessing to one you have hurt or sinned against can sometimes be a tricky proposition. Where you have violated the respect, trust, or rights of another, that person may or may not want to hear a confession. One offender described confessing as "like opening a boil," and you need to be sure everyone is ready before you open a boil. If the other person has a closed heart, he may prefer to see you suffer rather than give you the relief of a confession.

If you want to make things right, however, you will probably have to make the first move when you believe the time is as good as it is likely to get. Knowing when to bring up the past, and when not to, requires an insight and understanding of yourself and the other person. Confessing at the right time—when both you and the one to whom you are confessing are ready—helps you choose the right words and tone and improves your ability to listen to the other person's response.

When is the right time? Only you can say. Be sure to understand enough about the situation to raise the issues you need to raise and the other person needs to hear. Think deeply about what has happened and be prepared to be honest and communicate in detail about your behavior and its consequences. From the other person's perspective, try to decide whether he is prepared to accept your confession and respond in a helpful way. Does he trust you to be honest, is he willing to listen, can he rationally consider what you say? Consider the possibility that your confession will actually hurt your relationship if the other person isn't ready to hear you out. Only you can decide.

Don't use your concern about such considerations as an excuse for not doing what needs to be done. Err on the side of confessing when you can do so honestly. Confessing will usually work.

How to Confess

Each offender has two specific opportunities to confess during the Bridges To Life experience: when she tells her story, and when she writes two required letters, one to a victim (not sent) and one to a family member (sending is optional). The letters bring together all the offender has learned about herself and the Bridges To Life process. But they are mainly confessions. The story and letter of a prodigal daughter at the Henley unit just outside Dayton, Texas, tells us a lot about the power of confessions and how to go about them.

Lornita cried huge tears as she told her story to her small group, and other members from time to time gave her swatches of scratchy prison toilet paper to wipe them away. Lornita is an attractive but slightly mousy, petite twenty-six year old with flowing brunette hair, deep-set, sad brown eyes, and a curved button nose. She grew up in San Antonio, along with an older sister and two older brothers. Her father worked for many years at a local construction company, and her mother worked part-time in a day-care facility. Both parents were loving caretakers, although her father was a little stern and controlling at times, at least through Lornita's eyes. The family was a fixture in church on Sunday morning. Money was not overly abundant, but they had everything they really needed.

Lornita somehow got off track. In junior high she began slipping out at night and partying with older boys. She started smoking, drinking, and shacking up with her boyfriend. He introduced her to marijuana, then cocaine, got her pregnant, and then dumped her. She got an abortion without her parents' knowledge, struggled in school, and dropped out in the middle of the eleventh grade. Within a year she was pregnant by another man, a member of a local gang, and ultimately had three children by him. She had too much pride to ask her parents for help, so she supported herself dancing in strip bars and dealing drugs. She has been in and out of various correction facilities in the local area and has been in prison for two years, this time for delivery of a controlled substance.

Lornita's parents are caring for her children while she is in prison, but she has not talked to her father for the entire time. They have no communication, even though she occasionally can see him through a window when he brings her mother to prison for a visit. Lornita became visibly upset when talking about her father: how she had disappointed and hurt him, how she loved him, how much she would like a reconciliation that she didn't see as possible, how their pride was keeping them apart.

Lornita wrote a powerful letter to her father as part of the Bridges To Life experience. She for the first time confessed the abortion and told her father what he already knew—that she had been a stripper, drug addict, drug dealer. She acknowledged how badly she had hurt him and asked for his forgiveness. She committed to correct her life. When she read her letter to her group, her fellow Bridges To Life participants encouraged her to send it to her father. After a difficult wrestling match with her pride, she did.

Lornita's father attended the Bridges To Life graduation ceremony and for the first time in over two years talked with his daughter, hugged her, and cried with her. That night Lornita went to the microphone and read her letter to her father, in the presence of the entire Bridges To Life group and guests. The power of her confession worked God's miracle.

Lornita's confession provides several lessons. The first is to be fully accountable. Remember, as discussed earlier, that being accountable is necessary before confession. If you accept responsibility and are accountable, you have the power to set things right. Confess first to yourself and affirm your responsibility. Take full responsibility, be fully accountable to the other person, and don't try to deny what you have done or rationalize away the consequences. Do not shift blame or assign excuses, as this will only begin a negative cycle and make matters worse. There very rarely is a place for the word "but" in a confession. Do as Lornita did. Tell it like it is.

Your confession also needs to be specific. Like Lornita, most offenders have hurt the person to whom they are confessing—given him a sense of failure, embarrassed him, cost him money and time, prevented him from realizing his full potential, or committed other hurtful acts. The past cannot be changed, but simply saying a blanket "I'm sorry" will do little to restore the trust and potential that formerly existed. Trying to confess with generalities and trite remarks seems insincere and leaves the other person to wonder whether the confessor really understands what he is doing or is being honest about it. Generalities and often-used comments build cynicism rather than trust, push apart rather than bring together, hurt rather than heal. Confessions need to be detailed, specific.

Lornita confessed with specifics. Her letter included references such as:

- I aborted your grandchild, and I worked as a stripper, and I did drugs.
- I realize that I hurt you. I hurt you by embarrassing you before family and friends and making you feel you had failed as a father.
- I am responsible for this hurt because my actions, and not what you did, were the cause of our alienation.
- I am sorry because I love you and realize and acknowledge how my actions have hurt you.
- I want to be accountable to you by reconciling with you and maintaining a relationship where you can be proud of me.
- I am repentant, and I will turn my life around when I am released.
- I ask for your forgiveness.

Learn from Lornita. Be specific in your confessions.

The third lesson from Lornita's confession is to demonstrate humility. If you approach a situation with arrogance or let your pride show, your confession will not work. What is it like to be humble? Paul tells us in Philippians 2:3-7:

> Don't be selfish; don't live to make a good impression on others. Be humble, thinking of others as better than yourself. Don't just think about your own affairs, but be interested in others, too, and in what they are doing. Your attitude should be the kind that was shown us by Jesus Christ, who, though he was God, did not demand and

cling to his rights as God, but laid aside his mighty power and glory, taking the [form] of a slave and becoming like men. And he humbled himself even further, going so far as actually to die a criminal's death on a cross.

Lornita was humble enough that she read her letter to her father in front of approximately 100 people—friends and strangers alike. She did not try to cling to her rights, but laid her soul bare to her dad and confessed what she had done.

An effective confession also shows respect to the other person—the one to whom you are confessing. Respect is the other side of humility, as it involves how you see the other person rather than how you show yourself. Respect means treating the other person as you would want to be treated. It means being as sure as possible that she will receive a confession, perhaps asking permission before proceeding, acknowledging her humanity and the fact that she may be, probably is, hurting as well. Showing respect often means understanding that your confession is not as much about what you did as it is about how you affected her.

Lornita showed respect by getting over her pride and taking the initiative. She acknowledged that she was accountable to her father because he was her father and she loved him.

Confession requires you to be honest with your emotions. True confession is an emotional experience, both for you and the other person. Confession usually involves guilt, shame, fear, uncertainty, pride, pain, and other feelings: all emotions Bridges To Life participants demonstrate when telling their stories and reading their letters. Don't deny this fact or try to hide it. Let your honest emotions show and accept those of the person you are confessing to. If you don't honestly feel any emotions, don't try to manufacture them. Consider whether you can sincerely confess, or whether you should spare both of you from aggravation and move on.

During Lornita's confession the pain and suffering were obvious on her face. Her tears couldn't be restrained. Her father responded with tears and loving hugs.

Finally, when confessing use whatever approach fits. Nothing is better than a face-to-face confession, where the emotion can be felt, the tears observed, the person hugged. But sometimes a letter, phone call, or e-mail is more appropriate. Offenders often don't have an option—they are locked up, living away from a loved one, or otherwise prevented from making a face-to-face confession.

Confessing by mail will sometimes be more effective than other choices. Doing so gives you time to choose your words carefully, and it gives the person to whom you are confessing time to reflect, think about your confession, and perhaps pray about it before responding. As is often the case, you need to think about your own situation and do what you believe is best. Lornita sent a letter because she had no other option and, furthermore, was afraid her father would reject her and didn't want that to happen in person. Her letter of confession was accepted, and a written confession might be best for you as well.

STUDY QUESTIONS

1. How is your life like the prodigal son of Luke 15 and Lornita, the prodigal daughter? What do you learn from this prodigal son and daughter?

2. What does "confessing to your self" mean? How can you go about it?

3. Considering your own religious beliefs, how should you confess to your God?

4. How should you deal with those who have hurt you and should confess to you?

5. Think again about someone you have hurt or a problem you have caused. List all those to whom you should confess for your part in this situation.

6. Think about one of the people in Question 5 to whom you should confess. Is confessing now the right thing, or would it do more harm than good? Is this person able and willing to accept a confession? When is the best time to confess to this person? What is the best way for you to confess? In person, letter, phone, or another way?

7. Lornita's confession provides several lessons about how to confess. Which lesson do you believe to be the most important?

9

REPENTANCE

"Change gotta come within each man. Each man's gotta make up his mind."
Inmate, Walls Unit.

Claiming to repent—to radically change your life—is easy when you are incarcerated. Any change that gives hope for a better life is tempting. Think about it: being locked up on the Texas Gulf Coast in August without air conditioning, in a sweltering, poorly ventilated cell or dormitory where the air never stirs and the temperature exceeds 100 degrees, and you finally drop off to sleep each night in a pool of sweat. The tasteless monotony of badly prepared potatoes, beans, corn, and ground meat served day after day on a cardboard or plastic tray with plastic spoons and forks, and sometimes only peanut butter and jelly on stale rye bread for days on end during lock-downs. The fear of intimidation and possible assault. The depths of loneliness with absolutely no privacy. Hoping against hope for a letter or a visit from a parent, spouse, child, or friend and being disappointed when they don't come through. Having a visit from your children and not being able to show them where you live or adequately explain why you're locked up and can't go home with them. Having a visit from your spouse and returning to your cell frustrated with unmet longings or fears about what's happening on the outside. Having your life controlled by prying correctional officers. The indignity of strip searches, or even body cavity searches. The destroyed hope of rejected parole applications. The lack of freedom and hope in a country based on individual freedom and opportunity.

Under these conditions most offenders claim to repent, and "jailhouse religion" as a form of self-preservation is not uncommon. Think for a minute about repentance from Gilbert's point of view. Gilbert is a bright, engaging thirty-three-year-old in the Kyle unit. He grew up in a military family, lived in several different countries, and completed two years of computer science at a major university. He is now in prison for computer fraud. Gilbert has "repented"—made a commitment to himself to reform and never again engage in such criminal activity. However, he has made this commitment only because prison has achieved its goal of deterrence and social control. Gilbert doesn't plan to commit computer fraud again because he doesn't want to visit the big house again. He doesn't like prison, so he plans to stay away from crime when he is released, but he has no remorse for what he has done and no plan to make amends beyond what is necessary to minimize his time in "this hell-hole."

Juries, judges, prison officials, and others responsible for determining the type and amount of punishment for a crime typically consider whether an offender is remorseful and committed to change. Repenting, it seems, often leads to lighter sentences or earlier paroles, and this expectation raises the possibility of "jailhouse conversions," or insincere repentance in the offender's immediate self-interest.

Sometimes prison helps a person change who he truly is, because it removes the offender from his bad environment and provides an opportunity for him to really think about his life—but not in Gilbert's case. He doesn't see that stealing from a large corporation has hurt anyone and therefore has never really accepted responsibility for the consequences of what he did. And without accepting responsibility, true repentance is impossible. He has not had a change of heart or developed any sense of moral or spiritual rebirth.

That's where Bridges To Life can play a role for you—a role not related to your self-interest in minimizing time in your current situation, but one which appeals to your sense of humanity by creating a desire to change your life—to repent—and do the right thing in the future.

ABOUT REPENTANCE

It is obvious that as an offender you need to change your life. Your behavior has been so bad—so contrary to people's expectations or the community's laws—that you have been removed from the free-world society for a time. To gain peace with society you have to behave differently in the future. But simply changing your behavior is not enough. To restore peace with God and others, you must change who you are. You have to repent.

Repentance involves much more than a change of mind or behavior, or feeling sorry for one's actions. It is more than a jailhouse conversion or temporary change until the problems die down. True repentance is a transformation in which a person's fundamental character and being, not just his surface behavior, become permanently different. Repentance is the process by which humans leave their sins and bad behavior behind and radically and deliberately change their hearts and attitudes as well as their actions.

Repentance is a resolution that includes, but is more than, true remorse or sorrow for what one has done. A sincerely repentant person hates that aspect of himself that engaged in the hurtful behavior he now regrets. He is remorseful, sorry for what he did—not just sorry that he got caught—and each time he thinks of his wrongful act, he wishes he had made a better choice.

Paul described the sorrow of true repentance in 2 Corinthians 7:10: "For God sometimes uses sorrow in our lives to help us turn away from sin and seek eternal life. We should never regret his sending it. But the sorrow of the man who is not a Christian is not the sorrow of true repentance and does not prevent eternal death."

Richard Owen Roberts has described the sorrow of true repentance as follows:

[G]odly sorrow is concerned with the heart and soul rather than merely the body. Its quality of shame, pain, and agony of conscience may vary from season to season, but it will never totally disappear. It plumbs the depths of sin rather than merely scratching its surface. Because it goes deep, it may be less showy than the sorrow of the world, but once visible, it remains where all who care to see it can. [1]

When a person repents, deep remorse leads to a firm resolve to do better in the future, and she becomes a new person. Paul also wrote in his letter to the Ephesians:

But that isn't the way Christ taught you! If you have really heard his voice and learned from him the truths concerning himself, then throw off your old evil nature—the old you that was a partner in your evil ways—rotten through and through, full of lust and shame. Now your attitudes and thoughts must all be constantly changing for the better. Yes, you must be a new and different person, holy and good. Clothe yourself with this new nature. (Ephesians 4: 20-24)

Repentance is difficult and often not at all fun. C. S. Lewis described the process as follows in *Mere Christianity*:

In other words, fallen man is not simply an imperfect creature who needs improvements: he is a rebel who must lay down his arms. Laying down your arms, surrendering, saying you are sorry, realising that you have been on the wrong track and getting ready to start life over again from the ground floor—that is the only way out of our "hole". This process of surrender—this movement full speed astern—is what Christians call repentance. Now repentance is no fun at all. It is something much harder than merely eating humble pie. It means unlearning all the self-conceit and self-will that we have been training ourselves into for thousands of years. It means killing part of yourself, undergoing a kind of death. [2]

A simple story helps me understand what repentance is. I enjoy high altitude hiking—sometimes up to 14,000 feet—in

Colorado in the summer. Now, this is difficult for a "flat-lander" from Houston. Each climb is a long journey, with each step harder than the last, each breath more labored than the one before. My legs ache, my lungs burn. It's always easier to turn back, and often there is a great temptation to do so. But when I cross the treeless, windswept landscape of the alpine tundra and make it to the top, I am in a different world: a beautiful but desolate one with rocky talus instead of soil; short, scrubby arctic sage and alpine clover rather than pine or spruce trees, new and different critters and birds. Looking back, I can still see the world I came from, but I see it with an entirely different perspective. It seems smaller, less significant, behind me.

So it is with repentance. The journey of change, like climbing a mountain, is usually a difficult struggle, with temptations to quit or turn back. When you complete the journey, however, you are in an entirely new world that is very different from where you started. The old world is still there, but it is less significant, you see it differently. When you enter your new world, you have repented.

Repenting, like confession, admits you to the imperfect, fallible human race. Confession and repentance are acknowledgments of your own humanity and your need to change. Acknowledging one's humanity and mistakes enlarges one's capacity to love and provides a special understanding that makes forgiveness and reconciliation possible. Reasonable people can disagree about which comes first—confession or repentance. It probably doesn't matter. Confession involves acknowledging to yourself and others your need to change, and repenting is changing, whether or not the change is specifically communicated to others. Both free you from guilt and shame, foster personal happiness and emotional growth, and propel you forward on the journey toward becoming more Christ-like. Honest, sincere repentance enables other people to have confidence that you are a different person who will behave differently in the future.

Repentance is not a one-time event, but is an ongoing, daily, hourly attitude and change of life. Quoting Richard Owen Roberts again:

If someone comes to me with a report about repentance sometime in their past, I want to cry out, "So what? Who cares what happened years ago?" It is never enough to say, "I repented." You must be able to say, "I am repentant. Day in and day out, month after month, year after year, unceasingly, I live as a repentant person. I live in the spirit and attitude of repentance." 3

TRANSFORMING YOURSELF

Change is a process of moving from where we are, through a transition, to where we want to be. The Bridges To Life experience is a process intended to help you change your mind, heart, and behavior and become a trouble-free, law-abiding citizen. To do this, you will need to change from a "me-centered" life to an "other-centered" life.

Many—perhaps most—offenders have led troubled lives. You may have grown up in poverty, been abandoned or abused, and taught to violate the law rather than respect it. Even so, look honestly at your life and you will probably conclude that you have lived it for yourself—for "me"—when you didn't really have to. Have you focused on "poor me," and been disappointed that your life hasn't turned out as you hoped? Have you acted like Shane, who continually beat up on his little brother because it made him feel powerful? Or Ricki, who got drunk to satisfy his own desire to get high and have fun and killed a small child with his car. Or Lillie, who shoplifted from Walmart to fulfill her desire for drugs. Or Enrique, who burglarized over 200 homes because doing so was easier for him than working. Or Myra, who stayed in an abusive relationship because it permitted her to see herself as a victim rather than as a legitimate human being with a free will.

Bridges To Life aims to hold you accountable and show you the need for change: to get beyond "me" and start thinking about others and the larger society. It will help you understand that you exist for God and for his purposes, not your own, and that serving God's purpose means serving others. Repentance means transforming your life from a total focus on "me" and recognizing the humanity of those who have been truly victimized. It means appreciating the pain of victims and the needs of society, which strains under the personal and economic cost of disruptive and criminal behavior.

Focusing less on "me" and more on others will help you transform yourself and your relationships with others. To make such a change, you need to understand who and where you are, which is why it's no accident that the discussion of repentance falls where it does in the Bridges To Life process. Recall that the experience began with thinking about your story, examining your life, and taking responsibility for your inappropriate behavior. You then looked around and decided who you were accountable to. You then confessed to the person or persons to whom you are accountable. In sum, you've identified your behavior and admitted you were wrong.

The next step is change. If your focus, like most offenders, has been on yourself, you now realize you need to develop an "other" focus in your life and plan to transform yourself by emphasizing others. Listening, empathizing with others, embracing better choices, seeking God's help, and viewing repentance as a journey will help you with this process. Each of these steps to repentance is discussed below.

Listen

You can't change your focus from yourself to others without looking closely at yourself and caring about and understanding the needs of others. The best way to show that you care and to improve your understanding is to listen. You need to listen to God, to yourself, and to others.

Listening to God is necessary for repentance, because repentance is not just changing habits or behavior or turning over a new leaf because it's more convenient. True repentance is a moral and spiritual rebirth. We measure ourselves against the great moral code of our spirituality and find ourselves lacking. We deeply regret what we have done, and we aim to change in order to please God.

We can't know we need to change, however, unless we honestly listen to God and understand what he wants of us.

You probably have your own special way of listening to God, perhaps by reading and studying the Bible, communicating with Him through prayer, or listening to your pastor, priest, or other religious leader. Whatever approach you take, you should do whatever is necessary for you to genuinely hear what God wants of you.

Listening to yourself often isn't as easy as it seems, but it is important for two reasons: because you can enlighten yourself and because what you hear from yourself affects what you hear from others.

- Listening to yourself enlightens you. Recall from our discussion on accountability in Chapter 7 that one way we know right from wrong is that we feel it. How do we feel the difference? We listen to ourselves. We are the sum of our experiences, and our search for meaning and a new life has to start with self-knowledge—with knowing who we are and hearing those small voices inside our conscience that tell us who we should be. We can gain such insights only by listening to ourselves.

- Listening to yourself affects what you hear from others. Your beliefs, biases, and assumptions built up over a lifetime often prevent you from listening effectively, or they affect what you hear. They may lead to habits of negative responses, assumptions, labeling, or other ingrained acts that cause you to hear what you want to hear and suit reality to your own needs and wants. For example, Gilbert, introduced earlier in this chapter, believes big corporations have all the money they need and that they rip people off, so he had great difficulty hearing about the consequence of his computer fraud. In addition, what's currently going on in your life may distract you, cause you to pay attention to other priorities, or foster emotions such as anger, sadness, or frustration that detract from your listening.

Considerations such as these filter what you hear and may cause you to listen selectively, if at all, and react to a speaker in ways that tend to make a problem seem larger or smaller than it really is. For example, your anger about being left on your own may prevent you from hearing a parent's plea for understanding that she did the best she could.

To listen to ourselves we need to listen to our conscience—that small voice that tells us right from wrong and that we need to change. We also need to understand the filters that are potentially in our way and make adjustments if they are leading us astray. To listen to yourself, critically examine and understand your feelings, personal agendas, biases, and beliefs. Look objectively at what is going on in your world, discuss your conclusions with a friend, your spouse, or another adult, be receptive to new information and ideas, and make a conscious decision that even with difficult situations, you will respond to your own inner voice. For example, just acknowledging the stress in your life helps you see yourself as you really are and see that another person with a different point of view may have a legitimate point and is not just trying to hassle you.

Listening effectively to others requires a conscious effort to acknowledge and respect the other person, pay attention, and take in information. How well you listen now is affected by what you learned from your parents or from other life experiences, but listening nevertheless is a learned behavior. The key to learning is wanting to and intending to do it correctly. You can learn to listen better if you really care and will concentrate on it.

Listening to others is the foundation of the Bridges To Life small group experience, as offenders and victims of crime communicate and learn from one another. The communication is a two-way street, in which each person sends and receives messages in many different ways. Surprisingly, effective listening often does more to send messages than to receive them.

Listening is an effective way of sending information. Many messages from another person are really requests to "validate me," or confirm my self-worth by agreeing with me or at least showing that you value me and my ideas. You respond to these messages just by the act of how you listen, and how you listen tells the other person whether you are focusing on her.

When someone speaks, you cannot not respond, and even if you remain silent and show no reaction, you are still communicating. Failing to listen and respond effectively tells the other person something about herself and is likely to be seen as discounting her. If you ignore her, you are telling her that she isn't worth listening to. If you interrupt her, look stern while she is talking, or make snap judgments about what she is saying, you convey the message that she is stupid or uninformed. On the other hand, listening carefully to everything another person is communicating conveys the idea that she is valuable and worth listening to, and she feels validated. That's why listening is such an important part of the Bridges To Life small-group process.

Rachel Naomi Remen, in her book *Kitchen Table Wisdom*, says it better than I can:

> Listening is the oldest and perhaps the most powerful tool of healing. It is often through the quality of our listening and not the wisdom of our words that we are able to effect the most profound changes in the people around us. When we listen, we offer with our attention an opportunity for wholeness. Our listening creates sanctuary for the homeless parts within the other person. That which has been denied, unloved, devalued by themselves and by others. That which is hidden. [4]

An inmate from the Leblanc unit also made the point better than I can: "My family never came forward to hear me out, and it's a lot of offenders within prison who have a lot within themselves that family and loved ones has denied them to say, and I was able to get it out through Bridges To Life."

Effective listening also allows you to receive information from another person. You perceive what he wants or needs, how he feels, what he likes or dislikes, all the things you need to know in order to see yourself through the mirror of the other person and focus on him rather than "me." When you don't receive information properly, you will not respond appropriately, probably continue to focus on "me," and conflict or other problems are likely to result or continue. Listening effectively, on the other hand, allows you to learn where you are, whether you need to repent, and if so, how to go about it.

To take advantage of such lessons, you should suspend your own reality, try to understand the meaning behind another person's words, understand the other person's perspective, and accept that her feelings are justified from that perspective. You listen with your ears, mind, eyes, and heart, become aware of the speaker's feelings and emotions, and begin to see the world as she sees it. You separate the person from the words and accept the person as she is.

Thus, really listening to another person requires you to do much more than just be quiet and allow him to talk. You need to listen so you know how he feels, "walk in his shoes," and accept responsibility if you have caused problems. This is the starting point for developing the empathy necessary for you to repent and transform the focus of your life.

Empathize

You have empathy when you experience as your own the feelings of another. Empathy requires you to acknowledge your differences, control your own emotions, and put yourself in the other person's shoes. With empathy you are able to see her behavior from her point of view, react to bad behavior with love and understanding rather than unacceptable behavior, and make judgments about her behavior while avoiding them about her motives. You are able to see and understand how your actions have affected another person and feel true remorse for inappropriate behavior.

Creating empathy is at the center of the Bridges To Life experience. Danny, the twenty-four year old serving two twenty year sentences for vehicular manslaughter (introduced in Chapter 8) quickly develops empathy when he sits in the same small room with Kathy Connell and hears the story of her four children being killed by a drunk with a car. He sheds as many tears as she does. Dora, a thirty-two-year-old drug dealer with an eight-year-old daughter quickly develops empathy when Jan Brown tells the story of her nine-year-old daughter being murdered. You can see two mothers communicating.

Empathy is probably the most fundamental characteristic you need to put the "me" focus behind you and sincerely repent for your past behavior. Being empathetic requires you to move into another person's world with understanding and feeling. It goes beyond an intellectual understanding of what you've done, how you've hurt another person, and where you need to be. Empathy puts understanding into your heart and soul and allows you to feel the remorse that is necessary for true repentance.

The following ideas should help you empathize with another person so you can sincerely repent:

- Acknowledge that each of you has different beliefs, biases, and experiences. The other person's are his, they may be wrong or inappropriate, but they are his. To understand his, you have to deal with yours. You cannot understand that another person is different from you, with different feelings, beliefs, and needs, unless you know who you are and acknowledge your own feelings, beliefs, and needs. This is a threshold undertaking in the Bridges To Life experience. Could any two groups be more different than offenders and victims of violent crime? Yet, by acknowledging their differences, they begin the journey to mutual empathy.
- Listen empathetically and observe him and his behavior, as discussed in the previous section.
- Control your own negative emotions. You can't see another person's point of view if you are demonstrating frustration, anger, self-pity, or other negative emotions. If the other person's behavior is challenging you, reflect a minute, take several deep breaths, identify the emotions that are affecting you, and get yourself in control.

- Try to walk in his shoes. Think about him, his challenges, his fears, his pressures, his level of knowledge, how much information he has or doesn't have. How might you act in his situation?

- Identify with his feelings. When you are empathetic, you do not try to change the other person's feelings or necessarily understand why he has them. Instead, you try to feel as he feels, see what he sees, and appreciate the emotions that are present within him. Listen, observe, and feel in order to identify and appreciate his feelings.

Embrace Your Choices

Offenders often focus on "me" to such an extent that they consider themselves the real victims. This focus on "me" usually plays out in one of the ways discussed in Chapter 3:

- Thinking and acting from their own perspective and never considering the other person's

- Meeting their own needs and wants while disregarding those of others

- Abusing their power and control regardless of the feelings or welfare of others

- Demanding respect by using threats and fear

- Letting anger control them without regard to the feelings of others

- Feeding their addictions no matter what the consequences

Think about yourself and the extent to which you focus on "me" in one or more of these six areas, or in other areas unique to you. Now think about the choices you have and how you can focus less on yourself and more on others. Think about all the many ways you can change.

A Bridges To Life participant addressed the need for this type of transformation better than I possibly could. She explained it so well in a small group session that I asked her to write it down.

I honestly, truly and with all my heart, believe that we have choices in life. The same circumstances can happen to two different people, and those circumstances can be perceived in totally different manners.

When I was going through life as a "victim"—that's how I perceived myself—it was a period when I felt sorry for myself, wanted others to feel my pain, it was a stagnant period where there was no growth. After the last rape in 1997, I remember vividly thinking that my life would always be a series of "incidents"—and I awoke to the fact that EVERYONE has incidents in their lives, some more traumatic then mine, some less, but incidents nonetheless. I started studying how people reacted, how they carried themselves, how they perceived themselves, and discovered that those who were not only tenacious, but also had good self images, were the ones who seemed to be the most in control, the happiest, the most accepting. They were all different, but they all had one thing in common—they all served others by their experience. (Rape Crisis Center, Star of Hope, etc.)

I made a conscious effort to think of myself as a survivor. In the beginning, I literally would stand in front of the mirror every morning, and tell myself that I was a survivor, that I was loved by Abba, and that He had a special plan for my life! I didn't believe it at first, but I would say those words every day until I did. There are still days when I have to do self-affirmation.

Self-affirmation grew into the belief that is who I was—and slowly, but steadily, my self-image changed. As it changed, I developed real friendships, (after all, who wants to stay around someone who is whiny all the time!), a deeper love for Christ—and He directed me to serve others. Once I no longer felt the victim, no longer was self-absorbed, no longer felt sorry for myself; then, and only then, did the healing begin.

Today I'm a pretty happy person—I love my life, and I am blessed every day by the situations and people put in my path. Nothing seems so bad anymore—because I trust that God will not put anything in my path that I cannot handle.

We all have choices—no matter who you are, what you are, where you are, what you have done or haven't done— we are all special because we were given the incredible gift of choice. Sometimes those choices have the power to turn your life around—in my case, it was choosing to be a survivor AND a child of God—for others, there will be different choices to be made. But one thing we all have in common—when we stop focusing on self—that is the opportunity for amazing growth.

Seeing a better way, standing fast in our choices, and truly repenting can be very difficult, and we often need help. Fortunately, we can always depend on God's help.

Seek God's Help

Pamela is a forty-eight-year old daughter of the drug culture, with long, stringy, graying hair, a wrinkled face, knowing eyes, and a nose that's a little too large for her small face. Pamela is serving time for forgery. She explained through red, tear-filled eyes, "I can't connect the way most people do, so I just start by saying, 'Hey, J.C., what's up.' To me Jesus is a long-haired dude, wearing sandals, someone who looks like a hippie, someone I can connect to. He told me he wouldn't be around without the Father. I just try to be like Jesus, and remember that without the Father I wouldn't be around either."

Regardless of how you connect, like Pamela, you cannot really repent alone and you need the Father. Pray to Him as David did: "Create in me a new, clean heart, O God, filled with clean thoughts and right desires." (Psalm 51:10) Get beyond your focus on "me," ask for His forgiveness, and request Him to reveal your failures as they come, give you clarity to know what you need to do, and the strength to do it. God will do his part. You have to do yours.

View Repentance as a Journey

For many of us, repentance—leading a repentant life—involves changing our entire life. Think of Jermaine and how he grew up. He lived with his single mother in a poor area on the south side of Dallas. He can hardly remember a time when he wasn't in trouble. As a small child he ran away from home on several occasions, was found by police, and returned to his mother. In fourth grade he began skipping school to hang out with friends, usually smoking weed. The following year he was caught with a knife in school, helped set a fire in the gymnasium, and was involved in several fights. Jermaine was sent to alternative school—where he mainly learned more bad habits—and then to a juvenile facility for several days. In sixth grade he began smoking "wet" and joined a gang. The next year he stole a pistol from a friend's father and soon thereafter began a long series of assaults and robberies. He liked to get high on drugs, stake out an ATM, follow someone home, hit him in the head with his pistol, and take his money—which he usually used to buy more drugs. Jermaine is now twenty one years old, serving a long sentence in prison for aggravated robbery.

How does Jermaine hope to change from this entire lifetime of wrong-headedness and wrong-doing? He has to remember that repentance is not a one-time event, something that you do and then move on and forget about. Each time you repent, you take only one step toward a more lasting peace. Further, repentance is a journey of many steps, where you have to keep on keeping on. You have to keep on transforming yourself by continually listening, empathizing, focusing on better choices, and asking God for help. Each step is a challenge, often accompanied by difficult choices, embarrassment, and pain, and it's usually easier to just pass over the challenge than to repent. But even Jermaine, who needs to change from what he has become over his entire lifetime, can take the journey. He can look closely at himself, and change one thing at a time. And then another.

A letter from an offender at the Kyle unit just outside Austin summarizes this journey of repentance. Notice his acknowledgment of others and empathy with them, his move from focusing on himself to focusing on others, and his reliance on God for help in his journey:

To The Victims of My Crimes:

I have come to realize that through my drug use and drug sales and non-caring attitude toward society in general, I have hurt many people. To begin with, I want to apologize to all the children of parents that I had any drug dealings or drug use with. I know that I robbed you of many, many hours, days, months, and yes in some instances, from the time you were a toddler until you had reached adulthood, years of a safe environment and loving parents. I am responsible for the precious quality time that was taken due to addiction to drugs. I am writing this to ask you for your forgiveness, as God has forgiven me for my wrongs.

During the course of my drug use I was a really sick person who used to think that we all decide on our own to either use drugs or not. While that is true for most of us, I know now that many fall into drug use because they don't know how to live. They find escape from the pressures of life by medicating themselves and eventually that becomes their only way to survive. By putting drugs on the street I have been a driving force between broken homes, broken families, lost productivity in the work force. Drug use even affects the way neighborhoods grow and prosper. The drugs I put on the street cause crime to run rampant, our tax dollars are stretched to the point that eventually our government and civic leaders don't know what to do about it.

Just by my becoming repentant and accountable to my neighbors, my police force, and to the parents of children everywhere, this world can be a better place. By my admission of my wrong doings, I pray for forgiveness and through my actions, I intend to make my hometown a safer place for us all to live.

Through Kyle New Vision and the Bridges To Life programs, I now have the tools and insight to be a testament of triumph; not tragedy. I can and will now behave with compassion, respect, and dignity. I now have hope instead of hopelessness, and by the grace of God I am once again a caring, responsible member of society.

Sincerely from the Heart,
Charles

STUDY QUESTIONS

1. Describe the change you need to make in yourself to lead a truly repentant life as discussed in this chapter.

2. What help should you ask for from God as you try to live a repentant life?

3. Describe a person who thinks about "me" most of the time and rarely considers others.

4. Describe a person who cares for "others" most of the time and tries to meet their needs.

5. Which description best fits you—a selfish person who thinks mostly about self or one who cares about others?

6. Which of the ideas listed in this chapter is most important to you in developing empathy?

7. Arrange these topics in the sequential order that you think is best before repentance can occur: compassion, guilt, confession, remorse, sorrow, empathy.

8. Who do you need to listen to in order to see yourself as a survivor rather than as a victim?

10

FORGIVENESS

"I had a problem asking people to forgive me and I still have a slight problem because of all the bad things I've done. But I'm really and truly sorry, and I ask for your forgiveness."
Inmate, Hughes Unit

Manasseh was the son of Hezekiah, one of the most beloved kings of Judah. Manasseh became king of Judah when he was only twelve years old and reigned for fifty-five years as one of the most evil of all kings. Manasseh consulted spirit-mediums, fortune tellers, and sorcerers; encouraged his people to worship the idols of the heathen nations; and rebuilt heathen altars for worshipping the sun, moon, and stars in the very place where the Lord had said He would be honored forever. Manasseh sacrificed his own children as burnt offerings, and tradition has it that he probably gave the order to have Isaiah the prophet sawn in two. He encouraged every sort of evil, even seducing Judah and the inhabitants of Jerusalem to do more evil. As Bridges To Life offenders might say, "He was a bad dude," and he made God very angry.

After Manasseh was defeated in battle and taken prisoner he cried out to God for help, humbling himself and asking for mercy and grace. "And the Lord listened, and answered his plea by returning him to Jerusalem and to his kingdom! At that point Manasseh finally realized that the Lord was really God." (2 Chronicles 33: 1-13) Manasseh, a sinful man who did many evil things, asked for forgiveness and God forgave him. His story provides the context for this chapter.

Forgiveness is granting free pardon or giving up resentment for a hurt or debt against us. It involves looking back at what happened but not for the purpose of analyzing, blaming, or condemning. Forgiveness looks back for the purpose of leaving the offense behind and moving on to a better future. Doing so does not change the past or the bad things that have happened, but it does change the present and can change the future.

Forgiveness allows you to overcome intense negative reactions such as resentment, anger, hatred, and desire for revenge, which are caused when one has been wronged by another. It is "the feeling of peace that emerges as you take your hurt less personally, take responsibility for how you feel, and become a hero instead of a victim.... Forgiveness is the experience of peacefulness in the present moment." [1]

Forgiveness is a matter of the heart, the inner self, that involves a change in internal feeling more than a change in external action. "Forgiveness is the highest form of love, because it is love that maintains itself in the face of rejection and injury, that is, in the face of an enemy. People think that forgiveness of enemies is very radical, but it is only our enemies we can forgive." [2]

A variety of studies have shown that forgiveness is helpful to our health. Anger, blame, holding grudges, guilt, and shame are seen as contributing to heart problems, and people who fail to manage such feelings and emotions have higher incidences of heart disease and suffer more heart attacks than those who effectively manage their feelings and emotions. On the other hand, dealing with such hurtful emotions by forgiving or being forgiven leads to improvements in the cardiovascular and nervous systems. Forgiving increases our positive emotions and feelings of hope, care, affection, trust, and happiness and helps develop a better spiritual view, all of which contribute to physical health and improve our ability to deal with pain.

Forgiveness cuts both ways and is a choice, because it is a decision and an internal change of heart, not an action or behavior.

Sometimes you need to ask for forgiveness, and sometimes you need to grant it. However, you and I do not have to forgive anyone who has offended us, and people we have offended do not have to forgive us. No one can force you to change your mind and heart, no one can force you to forgive or ask for forgiveness or accept forgiveness, and no one can prevent you from forgiving. You have to decide what you will do, and others have to decide what they will do.

The sections that follow will help you decide when you should ask for forgiveness or forgive another and give you some ideas as to how to go about it. The first section focuses on God's forgiveness, the second on forgiving yourself, and the third on forgiving one another.

GOD'S FORGIVENESS

God forgave Manasseh, even with all his evil deeds, and He surely will forgive us when we have done wrong. We are all sinners. We often are unable to see ourselves in that light, but we are part of the human condition in which we are neither angels nor animals. Human beings have great capacity for evil, and some work very hard at becoming sinners, but we are made in God's image, He loves us, and no one is beyond His forgiveness. The Apostle Paul wrote in Romans 3:23-24, "Yes, all have sinned; all fall short of God's glorious ideal; yet now God declares us 'not guilty' of offending him if we trust in Jesus Christ, who in his kindness freely takes away our sins."

We should remember three important points about forgiveness. First, we all need to feel remorseful for our sins and continually seek forgiveness from God and our fellow human beings. We are badly mistaken if we see ourselves as morally or spiritually pure and others as evil. Acknowledging our sins does not reduce the effect of our offenses. It does acknowledge, however, that we are all offenders even if our offenses do not cause as much hurt or have such dire consequences as some that other people commit. We hear this point made time and again in Bridges To Life small groups, where victims of crime tell offenders, "but for the grace of God, I would be in white as well." We all need to be remorseful, and we all need to ask for forgiveness.

Second, all of us, even those who are guilty of terrible wrongs, are precious children of God, created in his image. Within all of us is a soul that has redeeming virtues. God loves all of us and is willing to forgive those who seek his forgiveness.

Third, God has placed a condition on His forgiveness that requires us to have mercy on our fellow human beings and those who have offended us. "Your heavenly Father will forgive you if you forgive those who sin against you; but if you refuse to forgive them, he will not forgive you." (Matthew 6: 14-15) More about this in the last section of this chapter.

Thus, God's forgiveness is available to all of us, and with His willingness to forgive it seems the rest should be easy. It isn't, however, so let's move to forgiving yourself.

FORGIVING YOURSELF

Ronnie's story is in several ways like Manasseh's. Ronnie grew up in a comfortable, storybook home. He was the youngest of three children living with both parents on a farm just outside a small town in northeast Texas. He has fond memories of hiking the fields and meadows, fishing, playing baseball, riding horses. His parents were conservative, perhaps strait-laced, but not in an overbearing way, and he had a close relationship with his extended family, particularly Aunt Pat. Dad had a regular job and Mom was a full-time homemaker. The family attended church together regularly and was respected throughout the community.

During his early high school years, Ronnie began running with a bad crowd, drinking, experimenting with marijuana, and staying out all night. The more he did, the more he wanted, the more he realized that he needed money, and the less he cared about how he financed his lifestyle. He began to use methamphetamines because they gave him the high he was looking for and he could manufacture them cheaply in his parents' kitchen with inexpensive ingredients purchased at Walmart.

Ronnie graduated from high school and that summer got his own apartment and a live-in girlfriend. This allowed him to avoid his parents more easily and step up his meth production. He supplied his own ever-increasing need and sold meth to users in the surrounding community. He developed a reputation for the high quality of his products and made enough money to live the "good life," which of course he couldn't enjoy because he was nearly always strung out on various drugs and out of his mind for days on end. He began to have trouble with the law—traffic violations while under the influence, using drugs, selling. After being arrested several times, he plea-bargained a twenty-year sentence in the Texas Prison System. He is now approaching parole after serving seven years.

Ronnie has had time to think while in prison—to think about his life and how much of it he has wasted, how many people he has hurt, including himself, all the people he sold drugs to and the people they hurt, and particularly his parents. Ronnie's parents have stood by him throughout. They tried to counsel him before prison and they visit him frequently now, showing their forgiveness and love in every way possible. This is a mixed blessing for Ronnie. He needs and wants their forgiveness and love, but their forgiveness also makes his shame and guilt even greater when he sees the pain in their eyes and thinks about how badly he has hurt them.

Ronnie knows his parents have forgiven him and he knows God has forgiven him. He wants to forgive himself, because he believes he cannot change his life unless he does. But doing so seems hypocritical, as he feels he has failed in so many ways. The following portion of a letter that Ronnie wrote to his family shows his remorse but also his struggle with forgiving himself:

> My throat is sore from the lump in it. Knowing every time I dream of either you or Aunt Pat, my very being breaks down. Aunt Pat, every time I think of the last time I saw you I weep out of remorse and still at times shame. I am so sorry. As I look back at the last time I saw you I can now see you knew what I was doing. The last words I can remember hearing you tell me as your feet dangled on the

edge of the ground from you sitting on your bed with the tubes that brought oxygen to your lungs was "Ronnie, you know I love you." It breaks my heart knowing the reason I went to your house was to get some new syringes so I could shoot more dope. You knew it and you told me you loved me. I wish I could make it up to you but I can't. From what I've been told I was the last person to see you alive. Monica found you two days later on the couch dead. I don't think I can ever forgive myself. The closest I can come to making this up to you is a living amends. I have finally sobered up that's a start.

Can Ronnie really forgive himself? Does anyone have the right or authority to forgive himself for hurting others? Reasonable people might disagree. Remember, however, that God will forgive you and you can accept God's grace and His forgiveness after you have confessed and repented to yourself and to God. Unless your standards are higher than God's, can you not forgive yourself? God forgives his children and we are all free to accept and live with His forgiveness. In the Bridges To Life experience, this living as forgiven persons allows participants to forgive themselves.

It seems to Ronnie that forgiving himself for his failures and all the hurt he has caused to Aunt Pat, his parents, to others, and to society is the same as saying what he did was okay, and he knows it wasn't. Feeling guilty and ashamed feels better than feeling forgiven, so he is trapped in his own guilt and shame over what he did in the past. Since he cannot forgive himself, Ronnie feels paralyzed and unable to get beyond his past to a better future. Instead, he is stuck "hoping for a better past."

Our need for self-forgiveness arises when we conclude our own behavior has been so unacceptable that it leads to some level of self-hatred. Self-hatred typically does not arise from some abstract notion of having defied a legal or moral law. Few offenders are deeply pained by such facts. Self-hatred often does occur, however, when we fail to meet our own expectations of ourselves or live up to our own standards, and do things that we regard as wrong and shameful. Failing ourselves rarely stands alone and nearly always leads to the second cause of self-hatred, which is when we hurt someone we love. Time and again offenders can forgive themselves for violating the law, but the rub comes where they have hurt themselves and someone they love. Ronnie, for example, was reluctant to forgive himself because:

- He didn't live up to his potential. He could easily have had his own automotive shop and be an important contributing member of society. Instead, he is completing his sixth year in prison as a drain on society.
- His own self-destructive lifestyle is a continuing burden. His use of drugs destroyed him. He had a choice in the matter but chose to become a blight on his community.
- He hurt so many people—his parents, siblings, friends, many unknown people who directly or indirectly suffered from the meth he sold. He hurt them both by what he did and by what he failed to do.

Thus, some people have difficulty forgiving themselves for their past behavior even after accepting responsibility, acknowledging accountability, confessing, and repenting. If you are in a similar situation, thinking deeply about the following should help.

- Accept that no one is perfect: we all make mistakes and bad decisions. Join the human race, where we all fail at some things and sometimes hurt other people. Accept that every mistake you have made probably has been made thousands of times by other people. Some do better, and others go further astray, but all of us need forgiveness. One of the great values of the Bridges To Life small groups is that offenders see firsthand that others, offenders and victims alike, are not angels either. Look around, and you will probably reach the same conclusion.
- Remember that forgiving yourself does not mean condoning what you have done. Some actions, such as murder or rape, are so evil that they cannot be minimized under any circumstances. Other behavior that causes problems, like under-age drinking or a

teenager skipping school does not seem quite so bad. The point to remember is that neither should be condoned, but both can be forgiven.

- Repent of your inappropriate behavior, as discussed in Chapter 9. Self-forgiveness without a commitment to change is a sign of nothing more than moral shallowness.

- Acknowledge your forgiveness. Forgiveness is a matter of the mind and heart: a decision you make and not what you do. Small group meetings in the Bridges To Life experience afford offenders the opportunity to discuss their concerns with others and in so doing acknowledge themselves and their forgiveness of themselves. You can take similar actions to solidify your forgiveness of yourself. Look in the mirror every morning and tell yourself you are a child of God, God has forgiven you, and you have forgiven yourself. Write a story of forgiveness and hope in your journal. Discuss forgiving yourself with a trusted friend.

We've discussed the easy part. God has promised his forgiveness, and we can control forgiving ourselves. But forgiving one another is often much more difficult.

FORGIVING ONE ANOTHER

Lisa, the youngest daughter of Patricia and Lee Stonestreet, was young, vibrant, full of vigor and hope: the essence of beauty and joy wherever she went and the apple of her father's eye. Lisa graduated cum laude from high school in Houston and attended Baylor University, where she made the Dean's List and was known as a popular, outgoing friend. After college she lived in an apartment in west Houston that Patricia, an interior decorator, had helped her decorate in a warm and welcoming décor that fit Lisa's personality. She loved her work as a legal secretary for the law firm of Vinson & Elkins.

Around two a.m. on a warm, humid June evening a drug addict high on cocaine broke into Lisa's apartment, brutally raped her several times, stabbed her in the eye, then strangled her and drowned her in her bathtub. The next day, Patricia tried to call her daughter, time and again, but got no answer. Anxious co-workers found her dead in the bathtub where her murderer had left her.

Are some people so evil that they are unforgivable? If so, would the murderer of Pat Stonestreet's daughter be in that category? Would you forgive him? Let me tell you what the Stonestreet family did.

The devastation of this vicious murder left Lee and Patricia's family and friends in tremendous turmoil—with gaping holes in their hearts as they continually asked the question, "Why Lisa?" The night after they buried Lisa, the Stonestreet family grieved together in their living room. Late in the evening, physically exhausted and emotionally spent, Lee and Vicki, Lisa's sister, at almost the same time felt the need for the family to collectively forgive Lisa's killer. Lee loved his daughter deeply and knew it would take God's help to accomplish such a difficult feat. He had a history degree from Rice, was a tri-captain of the football team and All-Southwest Conference center, was drafted by the NFL, and had faced many difficult challenges in his business career. He knew that forgiving this criminal would be the most difficult thing he had ever done.

The family decided that night that they would forgive Lisa's murderer but doing so at the time was just too difficult. At first their sadness, hurt, and anger won out. But over a period of nearly five years they became able to do so. Patricia, Lee, and Vicki eventually came to understand that they could forgive just the man himself, without forgiving what he had done to Lisa. Forgiving him freed the family, and they saw that forgiving is as important for those who are victimized as it is for the person who committed the crime. They realized forgiveness provides freedom from anger and bitterness and is the key to healing.

While forgiveness helped them heal, it did not help them forget. Patricia watched Lee, a man of great physical, emotional, and spiritual stature literally grieve himself to death because he felt he had failed to protect his daughter. Lee died, Patricia believes with a broken heart, on Lisa's birthday one year before her killer was executed. Patricia's memory of her daughter inspired her to devote her life to working as a volunteer for Bridges To Life. At the age of seventy-four she still traveled to prisons across Texas to share God's forgiveness with offenders and victims' families and had participated in more than twenty-five Bridges To Life programs. She said, "I find it personally healing to help prisoners understand the pain a victim and family members experience in a horrible crime, and I am encouraged to see many of their lives changed as they experience God's forgiveness through the ministry of Bridges To Life. It is emotional—yet rewarding—to read letters describing how they are now taking responsibility for their crimes." (Patricia died on December 17, 2009 after a long illness. The Patricia Stonestreet Volunteer of the Year Award was established in her honor, to be presented annually to a Bridges To Life victim volunteer.)

Patricia's story of evil, tragedy, faith, love, and hope sets the stage for our discussion of forgiving one another. Unlike accountability, responsibility, confession, repentance, and forgiving yourself, forgiving one another involves choices by both the offender and the victim. If you have offended someone and wish to be forgiven, whether or not the other person forgives you is her choice, not yours. If someone has offended you, you can choose whether or not to tell her you forgive her, and she can choose whether or not to accept your forgiveness if you do. Therefore, this section will deal with forgiveness from two perspectives: being forgiven and forgiving another.

Being Forgiven

We all want to be forgiven for our offenses and for hurting another if we are truly remorseful. Being forgiven by another is part of our healing process, and it helps us with our own self-forgiveness. It shows us that there is sufficient goodness in us that someone else has judged us forgivable and allows us to begin to find our peace. But we need to do our part if we hope for others to forgive us.

What did Lisa's murderer need to do to justify Patricia's forgiveness? What do you need to do if you have hurt or offended someone and need their forgiveness? The preceding chapters of this book have addressed these questions, as they have been leading toward the goals of forgiveness, reconciliation, and restitution. Briefly, they suggested the following:

- Prepare for forgiveness by being clear about the offense that is concerning you: understand specifically what you have done that is bothering you, making you feel guilt and shame, that requires forgiveness. Know how you feel about what happened, and how it is affecting you. A good way to do this is to tell your story to yourself, to a trusted friend, or to your journal.

- Accept responsibility for what you have done. You cannot accept another person's forgiveness if you deny that you are a cause of a problem or that your behavior has offended someone. Ask yourself why there is a problem, and why and why. If your name pops up, you probably need to accept responsibility.

- Assess who you are accountable to as a way of deciding from whom you need to seek forgiveness. If you have hurt or offended someone you are accountable to, then her forgiveness is important. You will probably conclude that you are accountable to God, to yourself, and to others. That's who you probably need to seek forgiveness from.

- Confess to God, yourself, and to others. Absent remorse and change of heart, we cannot appreciate forgiveness from God or others. We need to do our part. One of the primary objectives of Bridges To Life is to help you see that your actions have in fact hurt people you love, and that you need to develop an honest, healthy remorse for what you've done.

- Remember to repent. What story have you been living—the one where you see yourself as a victim, concerned only with "me," behaving badly? If so, what should your life look like instead? Are you committed to real change in your life? Can you now live a story of positive intention, optimism, and hope rather than bad behavior?

- Look ahead to restitution. We haven't discussed that yet, but it involves giving back, or making right the wrong you have done. Making restitution will go a long way toward helping with forgiveness.

More important, however, if we expect to be forgiven we have to forgive others. Jesus addressed this situation with the parable of the unforgiving debtor. A king discovered that one of his debtors owed him $10,000. The king tried to collect but the debtor couldn't pay, so the king ordered him, his wife, children, and everything else he had to be sold to cover the debt. The debtor begged for mercy, however, and the king was filled with pity and forgave his debt. The debtor then went to a man who owed him $2,000, grabbed him by the throat, and demanded instant payment. When the man begged for a little more time to pay, his creditor refused to wait and instead had him arrested and jailed until the debt was paid in full. When the king heard about what had happened he called his debtor before him and said, "You evil-hearted wretch! Here I forgave you all that tremendous debt, just because you asked me to—shouldn't you have mercy on others, just as I had mercy on you?" The angry king then sent the man to the torture chambers until every last penny was paid. (Matthew 18: 23-35)

C. S. Lewis in *Mere Christianity* has been quite explicit about his views concerning forgiveness:

> I am not trying to tell you in this book what I could do—I can do precious little—I am telling you what Christianity is. I did not invent it. And there, right in the middle of it, I find 'Forgive us our sins as we forgive those that sin against us.' There is no slightest suggestion that we are offered forgiveness on any other terms. It is made perfectly clear that if we do not forgive we shall not be

forgiven. There are no two ways about it. What are we to do? [3]

Thus, before asking for or expecting forgiveness, we need to forgive others. Think of Lisa's murderer. Could he have expected Patricia's forgiveness if he had refused to forgive those who may have contributed to his downfall?

Some final thoughts about being forgiven: Remember that forgiving you may be very difficult for the person you have hurt. Doing so may take time and effort. Empathize with Patricia's family, feel their pain, and think how difficult it must have been for them. Even asking for forgiveness might be considered an arrogant insult. Could you have faulted Patricia for feeling insulted if Lisa's murderer had asked for forgiveness soon after the incident? Thus, before asking for forgiveness, empathize with the person whose forgiveness you are seeking. Walk in her shoes and don't insult her.

Forgiving you is the other person's choice, and there is no way you can force it. He may be unwilling, at least at the time, to move beyond his anger, resentment, and other vindictive passions. He may feel that forgiving you compromises his sense of self-respect. He may believe that forgiveness requires him to make a moral compromise. Regardless of whether you agree with such attitudes, if he holds them they are his, and they will determine whether and when he will forgive you.

Asking for forgiveness is asking someone to do something important for you. You need to ask with humility and with respect because granting forgiveness is the other person's gift to you. Would you ask for another type of gift or favor with an arrogant, disrespectful attitude? Probably not, and you shouldn't ask for forgiveness with such an attitude either.

Remember that you can do all these things and still face a situation where those you hurt have not told you they have forgiven you: they may have, as it's a matter of the heart, but their forgiveness doesn't help release you unless you know about it. Patricia's family was aware of this. Before Lisa's killer was executed, the family made many attempts to speak to him and extend their olive branch of forgiveness as part of their own healing as well as his, but they were not permitted to do so in a direct way. They learned after the fact, however, that a compassionate chaplain had communicated their forgiveness to Lisa's killer before he died, and they were greatly relieved and thankful for the chaplain's action.

Finally, remember the power of asking for forgiveness. This power is eloquently demonstrated by a letter written by the wife of Jack, an inmate who, as part of the Bridges To Life experience, had asked for her forgiveness for all he had done and for the hurt he had caused. A portion is quoted below:

Baby:

First I want to say that I love you beyond words! Thank you for writing that letter to me. It was so weird but when I read it, I felt all the old hurt and anxiety flood out of my body. I felt such relief and I don't know why. I guess I just felt like verbalizing it washed it away. Thank you so much. You never needed my forgiveness, just your own and God's. You have His. I love you. As bad as the last 3 years have been without you, I guess God's purpose was to bring about the changes he was looking for in both of us. I believe he has succeeded. Thank you for your letter. It's the best one I've gotten from you. And I have a whole box of letters from you. We're gonna make it, Baby.

Thus, as with Jack, just asking for forgiveness often leads to new hope, a fresh start, a new beginning.

Forgiving Another

Sometimes we are the victim, and we need to forgive an offender. When Jesus was asked how many times we should forgive, he answered "seventy times seven," which seems to mean there is no end to our need to forgive. (Matthew 18:22)

Earlier in this section, I raised the question whether some evils and some people are unforgivable? At the extreme, think of Hitler, or in later times Saddam Hussein? Or the person who brutally murdered Lisa. Philosophers and moralists disagree, and some take the view that such people should not be forgiven and should be allowed to stew in their own juices. I will not try to tell you what you should believe in such extreme cases, but I will make two points.

First, I believe Patricia and her family were right in their decision to forgive Lisa's murderer. Their actions seem perfectly consistent with God's plan that we forgive in order to be forgiven. In addition, those who have been hurt benefit immeasurably from forgiving those who hurt them. Patricia and many other Bridges To Life victims have forgiven some very serious and brutal offenses and benefited greatly from doing so. The healing they received seems to confirm the appropriateness of forgiving the murderers who took their loved ones and caused them and their families so much pain and suffering.

More than anything, forgiving someone else helps your own healing process. Forgiving one who has hurt you will free you from being consumed by your anger, minimize any tendency you may have toward vengeance or vindictiveness, and set the stage for restoring any relationship that is worth restoring where you have hurt another and he wants to be forgiven. In the words of Pat Stonestreet's daughter, Vicki, "God in His sovereignty forgives man. Therefore, we are able to forgive others, even after something as devastating as the murder of our loved one. And forgiving is the thing that makes some degree of healing possible."

Paula Kurland, who also lost a daughter to murder (to be introduced in Chapter 11), put it this way: "I forgave Jonathan (her daughter's murderer), and he was gracious enough to accept my forgiveness. I left everything with him, and that gave me peace."

The second reason for rejecting the idea of not forgiving is that, to our great fortune, most of us don't have to face really extreme wrongdoing. The wrongdoing most of us face is ordinary by comparison to that faced by Pat, Paula, and other Bridges To Life victims. It seems clear that such ordinary wrongdoers, certainly if they show remorse and a change of heart, should be able to get on with their lives with some degree of forgiveness. That means you, the offended, should forgive them.

Thus, we can take it that we should forgive those who have offended us. Doing so isn't always easy, however, and there often is confusion about what forgiveness is and is not and how to go about it. The Stonestreet family experience can teach us a great deal in this regard. Let's start with lessons about what forgiveness is not or does not mean:

- Forgiving does not condone bad behavior. Some are concerned, for example, that forgiving a murderer is selling out or betraying the loved one who was murdered. When you forgive someone, however, you are not saying that what he did was right. You let him off the hook of any emotional obligation to you for what has happened, but you do not endorse what he did or say doing it again is acceptable. God's willingness to forgive us is a good example. He hates sin, but forgives us. Thus, in the words of Pat Stonestreet, "You can forgive the person without forgiving or condoning his actions or behavior."

- Forgiveness does not require establishing a close relationship. The Stonestreet family forgave the person who killed Lisa and wanted him to know of their forgiveness before he was executed, but they did not want to develop a friendship with him. Think about Ramona, whose ex-husband beat her unmercifully, caused the abortion of her unborn child, made her fix his breakfast the next morning, and berated her for getting blood on his car when he finally took her to see a doctor. Forgiving him can help Ramona deal with her pain, and she may well forgive her ex-husband. But re-establishing a relationship and living together again? No way!

- Forgiveness does not mean forgetting. That Texas philosopher, Willie Nelson, had it at least partly right when he sang, "Forgiving is easy, but forgetting takes a long time." Forgiving isn't always easy, but it does not mean we forget. It is getting beyond, not forgetting, denying, or minimizing. Pat and Paula and many other Bridges To Life participants have forgiven, done a lot of healing, and continue to heal, but they haven't forgotten what happened. That's one of the reasons they devote so much of their lives to Bridges To Life.

- Forgiveness is not the same as mercy, and it does not mean the offender should not pay the consequences. Patricia and her entire family forgave the person who murdered Lisa. But they did not fight his execution and in fact supported it as an appropriate consequence of his offense. Their actions can be explained in several ways. First, Patricia did not have the power or authority to exercise mercy. The state of Texas, not private individuals, executes certain murderers, and the state, not private individuals, has the power to grant acts of mercy. More importantly, Patricia did not advocate the punishment out of anger or vengeance or for any vindictive reason. Instead, she believed that execution was the only way to protect society from future acts of this individual and that the state's policy is an effective way to protect society from people like him.

We also learn several important lessons from the Stonestreet family about what forgiveness is and how to go about it. First, forgiveness should be unconditional, not dependent on the offender's actions. Pat's family decided to forgive the offender before he confessed his guilt, said he was sorry, or showed any remorse. Remember, Pat's husband said on the day of Lisa's funeral, "We've got to forgive this man," and difficult as it was, they did so. Our forgiveness of others cannot depend on their admission of guilt or wrongdoing. Recall the story of the prodigal son, discussed in Chapter 8. The father didn't have to wait for his son to confess or repent in order to forgive him. The father welcomed his son home as soon as he saw him on the horizon, before he knew whether or not he would confess and repent. His son's attitude didn't matter. He was forgiven.

This need to forgive a person whether or not he has shown remorse and repented involves a double standard of sorts, as I have earlier suggested that to forgive yourself and to ask for forgiveness from God and another, you need to show remorse and repent. The double standard is based on the fact that you can control your own actions but not those of another person. You can decide to confess and repent, but you cannot make that decision for someone else.

You can welcome confession and repentance from another person when it occurs, and even create a climate that encourages it, but you cannot force another person to do what you think she should do. She will act as she wishes, and trying to force confession or repentance is more likely to lead to lying and further destruction of your relationship than to moral and spiritual rebirth. If you want to forgive another person, but require him to take these actions before you forgive him, you are giving that person the power to control whether and when you forgive. You are giving this power to a person who has already hurt you and are allowing a double hurt: once in the original offense and the second when the offender obligates you to retain resentment and refuses to allow you the healing you can obtain by forgiving him.

The second lesson is that forgiveness can be very difficult. Although Patricia's family agreed immediately that they had to forgive Lisa's murderer, they needed over four years to get there. Their sadness and anger were just too great. Or let's jump ahead to Paula Kurland's story. Like Patricia, Paula's daughter was brutally murdered (the story is in Chapter 11), and Paula had great difficulty forgiving the man who did it. In her own words:

> I had a real hard struggle with forgiveness. I had a huge struggle with forgiveness, and I fought God every step of the way. It took seven years to get to the point that I could accept the fact that I had to forgive him. God had let me know that I did not have to forgive what he did, but I had to forgive him. So God had to separate him from Mitzi before I could even consider any kind of forgiveness. But it took another five years for it to come to fruition.

Because I still, I knew I had to, but I didn't want to. I just couldn't do it. But I did forgive him, but not what he did.

In more ordinary situations, forgiveness often is easier if you really think deeply about what happened and all the surrounding circumstances, as this often leads to a conclusion that the offense was not as bad as you thought. If you remind yourself that you are just one among many who have suffered such an offense, it may seem less significant. You probably are not the first, and you will not be the last. Remember that in most cases (unlike those suffered by many Bridges To Life victims) the offender did not intend to hurt you personally, and refusing to see an offense as a personal attack makes forgiving it easier. Don't minimize important things that have happened, but do place them in the right context.

The third lesson is that since forgiveness is an internal decision of the heart, you don't have to confront the offender you are forgiving, and he may or may not even know about it. Forgiveness does not demand that you communicate with the other person. It often is mainly for you and may take place, for example, after the offender is dead. Sometimes telling another you forgive her would be construed as arrogant and too judgmental, and the person would resent it rather than accept it. You may need, for your own reasons, to forgive someone for something she does not believe was wrong, for which she does not want forgiveness, or that she isn't even aware of. In such cases, communicating forgiveness is a form of accusing that may lay a guilt trip on the other person and not be appropriate. You are not the judge, so you don't have to confront to forgive. On the other hand, remember that telling someone you forgive him is often a powerful blessing to him. You decide and do what is right.

The final lesson from Patricia, "the rest of the story,'" is a living demonstration of God's requirement that there be no end to our willingness to forgive. Approximately six months after Lisa's death, burglars broke into Patricia's home and stole the diamond pendent she and Lee had given Lisa—the one that was around her neck when Lisa was murdered—along with other favorite family pieces. Patricia walked the pawn shops for a year looking for this piece of Lisa to hold on to, but she never found it.

Then, about three years later, burglars broke in again and took all her husbands memories: his awards, both their wedding rings, everything Patricia had to hold on to and cherish. Now she had nothing from either her daughter or her husband to comfort her. Patricia explained:

> When I came home that night from being out of town and realized I had been burglarized again, I sat on the floor and wept. I had been victimized again. The offenders were never caught, and I was left with nothing tangible to hold when I needed comfort, to remember my husband and daughter. I only had the good and bad memories tied with a purple ribbon and hid in my heart. As I sat there, I realized that I was faced with the same issue again about forgiveness. I had to forgive the people that did this to me, but it was so hard for me to think about it again.

STUDY QUESTIONS

1. Why do people so often refuse to forgive one another?
2. If you do not forgive one who has offended you, what happens to you?
3. What is the most important lesson from the story of Manasseh?
4. What does it mean to "forgive yourself?"
5. Why is it important for you to forgive yourself of your mistakes?
6. How do you know when to tell someone you forgive him or her?
7. What do we need to do before we ask for forgiveness from another?
8. Which experience gives you more healing—forgiving someone or being forgiven?

11

RECONCILIATION

"The only thing I can do is ask for your forgiveness and let you know if there is any amends or way to reconcile to you individually, please tell me."
Inmate, Ney Unit

Jonathan arrived at the small house in the Austin suburbs just before daybreak on a crisp September morning. He knew his way around, even in the dusk of early daybreak. Although he had never met the three people sleeping inside, he had been there so many times, stalking late at night, that Kelly's dog didn't bother to bark anymore. Jonathan quietly popped the latch on a double hung window in the kitchen, raised the lower portion, and crawled through.

Mitzi was awakened by the shrill, terrified screams from Kelly's room. By the time Mitzi got up and made it into the hall, Jonathan had already stabbed Kelly fourteen times with his six-and-one-half-inch hunting knife and slit her throat. When he encountered Mitzi, Jonathan stabbed her time and again all over her body. Mitzi screamed and yelled for Ronnie, who was asleep in a third room. When Ronnie found them, Jonathan had pushed Mitzi into a closet, where he was on top of her, continuing with his savage blows. Ronnie pulled Jonathan off of Mitzi, and Jonathan started stabbing him, in the eye first and then all over. Ronnie fought him down the hall, and in the process Jonathan cut himself, leaving his own blood among the carnage in the bedrooms, hall, and bathroom. Ronnie managed to get out the front door, and

Jonathan ran out the back. A neighbor called 911. Both girls were dead when help arrived, and Ronnie had almost bled to death.

In a matter of minutes, Jonathan stabbed Kelly fourteen times and killed her. He stabbed Mitzi twenty-eight times, and she bled to death from a cut of the main artery behind her knee. He stabbed Ronnie nineteen times and almost killed him.

After Jonathan left the scene of his slaughter, he called his girlfriend and told her he had been in a fight with a drug dealer and needed help getting rid of his blood-covered clothes. He cleaned up and, with help from his girlfriend, bandaged his wound, put his clothes, his knife, blood-splattered towels, rugs, even wallpaper from the house where he changed, into black trash bags. The two threw them into a vacant lot in the Austin hills, and by 9:00 a.m. Jonathan was at his boss's house, casually sitting by the pool drinking cocktails and talking about a business venture.

That September 13 was the first day of a hellish life for Mitzi's mother, Paula Kurland, her fifteen-year old daughter, Kyrra, her thirteen-year old son, Joey, Mitzi's father, her grandparents, and friends. Nothing would ever be the same. Mitzi was Paula's first child, the one with the open, guileless face, the pixie smile, the round sparkling eyes, the long, brunette hair curling softly over her shoulders. She was brutally murdered on her twenty-first birthday by Jonathan, an early-release parolee who had been out of prison for four months. He was a drug addict, serial rapist of four or five women—now a double murderer. That afternoon Paula watched the scene on television as Mitzi's body was removed from her house.

Paula Kurland is a Bridges To Life victim volunteer who, like John Sage and so many others, has devoted her life to helping offenders become accountable for what they've done and in the process healing herself a little at a time. Her story is a perfect demonstration of both the struggle that reconciliation often is and the power for healing that it can be.

Reconciliation means different things in different situations. We most often think of it as the coming together of two people, perhaps two who have been estranged, or refuse to talk with one another. But reconciliation means more and can address all sorts of differences between people, within yourself, and between you and God. It can mean restoring a broken relationship, but can also mean settling a quarrel or difference, reaching an agreement, changing conflict into peacefully getting along, winning over to friendliness, or reestablishing a loving, intimate relationship. Let's look at some important characteristics of reconciliation:

- Reconciliation is a choice, not something that is sure to happen. You can go through the entire Bridges To Life process and not reconcile unless you choose to do so and make an effort to cause it to happen. Since two are necessary, another person must also choose to reconcile.

- Reconciling is connecting, not winning. Reconciliation involves establishing a relationship that allows people to come together in some fashion and become more nearly whole, rather than stay apart and be less than whole. It focuses on win/win solutions and avoids relationships where one wins and the other loses.

- Reconciliation is growing, not giving in. When you give in you are controlled by another person's power. When this happens, you often experience shame, self-doubt, and self-hatred and respond to the other person's behavior with your own shallow exercise of power in the form of coldness, sarcasm, or other small signs of resentment. True reconciliation, on the other hand, allows a relationship based on strength, love, and wholeness in which both of you can grow and expand.

- Reconciling is a journey, not an event. It doesn't happen all at once and may take many years. Reconciling is a little like tearing down a brick wall by hand. Think of you and another person as being separated by a brick wall. You cannot get over it, go around it, or blast your way through it. The only thing you can do is to slowly, gradually break the mortar and remove one brick at a time and keep removing one brick at a time until the wall is low enough that you can get to the other side.

Reconciling is a similar process, where you and the other person tear down the things that are hurting your relationship, one step at a time.

- The destination of your journey of reconciliation can take one of many forms. Think of how your destination in reconciling with yourself, with God, and with another will all be different. Think of how your destination in reconciling with a person you barely know will be very different from your destination in reconciling with a spouse or parent.

Let's continue with Paula's journey. It took police almost a week to find and capture Jonathan, and then the wheels of the judicial process began their slow, creaky, never-ending movement. Five pretrial hearings were held during the year following Mitzi's death. Jury selection for Jonathan's trial started on September 14 and took a week. The trial lasted three weeks.

Those three weeks were unimaginably awful for Paula. She wanted Jonathan convicted, but at the same time wanted him to be represented well, so he wouldn't get off on a technicality or loophole. The worst part was watching Jonathan with his cocky, sinister attitude as he looked continually at Kelly's sister, who had a striking resemblance to her. As Paula said, "His eyes were cold and empty, and at the same time glowering and menacing. I could see nothing but evil in them. As Jonathan looked at Kelly's sister, I could see what he was thinking, and what he was thinking had already cost two lives. It made my stomach turn and my blood boil."

The jury convicted Jonathan of murder and assessed the death penalty. Paula was relieved but not happy. "I felt he deserved the death penalty, not because I wanted to see him die, but because I knew that was the only way to protect society from him and that I would feel secure that he wouldn't get out and do it again. The media couldn't understand why I wasn't happy."

At a very brief encounter during a pre-trial hearing, Jonathan quickly said to Paula, "I am sorry. I am so sorry. If I could give my life right now to bring her back, I would." Paula responded,

"That's just not enough." Paula tried to see Jonathan at the jail on the day he received the sentence to die. She wanted to say something to him, but arrived twenty minutes after he had been taken away to death row.

To say that things went downhill for Paula and her family from the time of the trial is an understatement. Mitzi's death, and Jonathan in particular, became Paula's focal point. She was not mentally or psychologically present for her other children because she occupied another world. Her kids suffered miserably and are still scared by the trauma of all the events. Their lives went on, but Paula isn't sure how. She was angry with Jonathan for murdering her daughter. She also was confused about why God allowed it to happen and had conflicting feelings that she didn't understand. She faced very difficult tasks: the tasks of reconciling with herself, her God, and Jonathan. And she didn't really know what reconciling would mean under such awful circumstances. Paula often wondered, "How can I forgive him when he took it so lightly?" In particular, Paula wondered what type of peace she could ever reach with Jonathan. But her life teaches us a great deal about reconciling with ourselves, with God, and with others.

RECONCILING WITH YOURSELF

It is difficult to reconcile with others until you reconcile with yourself. Doing so can mean various things, but above all it means being at peace with yourself. To gain peace with yourself, you need to recognize and acknowledge the conflict within your own being—confusion about who you really are, failure to acknowledge responsibility for your behavior, resentment or hatred toward others, guilt or shame for what you've done, emptiness or other destructive feelings and emotions.

Sandra is a good example of serious internal conflict and the need for reconciling with one's self. She is forty-two years old with small, dull eyes, crooked teeth, and a blank stare in her eyes. She appears very frumpy in her loose hanging prison whites, which occasionally reveal the multi-colored tattoo on her right forearm. Sandra has a history of drug abuse, selling drugs, and forgery.

Shortly before her current incarceration, she was raped by two stoned drug dealers while she was buying drugs for her abusive boyfriend. She says that her only mistake was having a coke pipe in her purse when the police arrested her for loitering at a bus stop, and that's why she is behind bars. Sandra cannot see herself as anything other than a victim of rape and unfortunate timing.

Without in any way minimizing the magnitude or consequence of the rape, it is accurate to say that she is an offender as well as a victim. She has never recognized the conflict between her life as a drug dealer and her life as a rape victim because she is denying so much of both. She cannot resolve this internal conflict and reconcile with herself until she is honest about her whole life.

At other times internal conflict has to do with circumstances such as your beliefs, the mental images that direct your life, or your priorities. You may be unclear as to right and wrong in many situations or feel undervalued because your parents said you were no good, or you may feel you hate your parents, or otherwise fail to focus on what is really important. In summary, there is a side of you that you like, and also a side that you don't like, and you need to reconcile the two. How many people do you know who have internal conflicts such as these? Perhaps a parent, a spouse, a friend, or the person you see in the mirror each morning. Most of us have some degree of internal conflict.

Sometimes resolving your internal conflict and reconciling with yourself is a long and difficult journey where you need help from a friend, spiritual advisor, or professional counselor. In simple terms, however, reconciling with yourself boils down to making peace with the part of you that you don't much like. Building peace—whether between people or within a person—is the purpose of *Restoring Peace*. Thus, all the preceding chapters have been telling you how to restore peace, or reconcile, with yourself. Let's briefly review important teachings of these chapters in this context, as a road map for a process that works.

- Remember that God loves you, will help you, and through Him there is hope. Pray to Him and seek His help in your reconciliation effort (Chapter 4).

- Clarify who you are, emphasizing the parts you like and the parts you don't like. Acknowledge responsibility for your behavior and its consequences (Chapter 6) and be accountable to your own conscience (Chapter 7). Be honest with yourself, look deeply within yourself, face up to issues you have previously avoided, and let yourself be confronted by others and your own conscience. Sometimes it helps to tell your story to another person who can listen with empathy, help you be honest with yourself, and hold you accountable. The small-group session in the Bridges To Life experience accomplishes this purpose, as the group holds each person accountable for what he has done and how he views himself. You can also confront yourself by writing in your journal or writing a letter to yourself.

- Be honest with yourself about the part of you that you like, the part that you don't like, and who you are. Sandra, for example, needs to look inside herself and decide whether she is a rape victim, a drug-addicted felon, or a whole person fashioned by both experiences, accountable for all her behavior. Confess to yourself about the part you don't like (Chapter 8). Remember that admitting our wrongs or internal conflicts to another person is an excellent way of confessing them to ourselves.

- Repent, or commit to change the parts you don't like. Think about the type of relationship you want with God and with your fellow human beings. Think about what peace means to you and the type of person you need to be to bring peace into your life. Pray for enlightenment. Establish goals for your life and then change the parts of you that don't contribute to those goals. You cannot change some parts of you, but you can change others. Sandra cannot change the fact that she is a rape victim; the pain and indignity of the assault will be part of her forever. She can, however, change the way she views herself. She can view herself as a whole person rather than part of one, a survivor rather than a victim. Similarly, you can repent and change who you are. You can quit identifying with the negative, hurtful, and worldly and begin to identify with the positive and the spiritual.

- Forgive yourself and get on with your life. God will forgive you, and you can forgive yourself.

Making peace with yourself is not an easy assignment, but you can do it with God's help, and when you do, you have reconciled with yourself. You are then ready to move on.

RECONCILING WITH GOD

The Apostle Paul, in Romans 5: 6-11, provides an example of how God reconciles himself to us and how we can be reconciled with Him by being His friend:

> When we were utterly helpless with no way of escape, Christ came at just the right time and died for us sinners who had no use for him. Even if we were good, we really wouldn't expect anyone to die for us, though, of course, that might be barely possible. But God showed his great love for us by sending Christ to die for us while we were still sinners. And since by His blood he did all this for us as sinners, how much more will he do for us now that he has declared us not guilty? Now he will save us from all of God's wrath to come. And since, when we were his enemies, we were brought back to God by the death of his Son, what blessings he must have for us now that we are his friends, and he is living within us!
>
> Now we rejoice in our wonderful new relationship with God—all because of what our Lord Jesus Christ has done in dying for our sins—making us friends of God.

What does it mean to be a friend of God? That's a question about which volumes could be written. Let's think, however, of a few simple characteristics of our own friendship with other people and see what it tells us about how we can reconcile with God.

- Friends have affection for one another. God has done His part on this point. We all are His children, He has an unconditional love for us, and He has made clear His willingness to forgive us for our offenses. We are not perfect, and never will be, but we all have the ability to walk with Him and try to live in harmony with Him. The choice is ours, and all we have to do is act.

- Friends are not here today and gone tomorrow. Nothing stands in the way of their relationship, and they stick it out through thick and thin, are not alienated or estranged, and don't hold grudges. The same is true if you are God's friend. Paula and other Bridges To Life participants have experienced some incredible lows in their lives—lows that could have caused them to forsake their friendship with God. They accepted God's will, however, and their friendship with Him grew even stronger. We all should follow their example.

- Friends communicate by listening to one another and talking with one another. They ask one another for help. Communicating with God means reading and studying His word and talking to Him in prayer. Turning to God in love and humility can be the foundation for your friendship with Him. You ask for His help and thank Him for it. You acknowledge your true condition, recognize His incomparably greater power, and give Him room to work in your life.

- Friends try to please one another, and each goes out of her way to do what the other wants. If we are God's friends, we aim to please Him and do what He wants us to do rather than what we would like to do. We surrender to His will and please Him by living for His purpose, abiding by His commandments, and giving Him the glory.

These four simple principles of friendship—showing affection, maintaining the relationship through all the ups and downs, communicating through prayer, and pleasing God by surrendering to his will—will go a long way toward your reconciling with God and pave the way for your reconciliation with human beings.

RECONCILING WITH ANOTHER

Reconciling with another is rarely easy, and it usually begins with forgiveness: asking for, giving, or both. Paula's long and difficult struggle with forgiveness was recounted in Chapter 10, and it was only a start toward the more difficult task of reconciliation.

Paula had been trying to see Jonathan for the entire time he had been on death row. She says:

> I have no idea why I wanted to see him. I had to sit and talk with him and I didn't know why. It was just something I needed to do. Even now I don't know why—probably to let him see what he had done and what he had left behind. I just had this deep need. My family thought I was crazy. You are torn apart from the whole world, isolated like no other isolation you can imagine. You are just there. Your thoughts, words, and deeds have no meaning anymore. In retrospect, I was trying to regain some control back into my life.

About a dozen years after Jonathan's conviction, David Doerfler of the Victim Services Department of the Texas Department of Criminal Justice contacted Paula. He offered the Victim Offender Mediation Dialogue (VOMD) process and asked if she wanted to participate. He explained that the process is a unique program that permits victims to request a structured, face-to-face meeting with "their" offender. The offender volunteer must admit guilt before the meeting, and the mediation is not part of an offender's parole file, which assures that offenders do not participate in order to enhance their chances for parole. The idea is that through VOMD victims may receive answers to unanswered questions, which helps in their healing and recovery process. It also permits offenders, in the truest sense, to acknowledge that they are responsible and accountable for their own behavior.

Participation in VOMD normally takes months of preparation, but Paula was ready because she had been trying for years to gain contact with Jonathan. This was an answer to a twelve-year prayer and, she hoped, a turning point for her in her continuing efforts to gain a little bit of peace.

Paula described her experience as she sat face to face with Jonathan, only a glass partition separating them:

> The purpose is not for the victim to go in and beat up on the offender. It's to tell him how you feel, and the offender has to take full responsibility, because if he doesn't, letting the victim in is just a re-victimization by the system. Jonathan had to convince me he was sincere. I knew I had to tell him he was forgiven before he died. It would be God letting me off the hook.
>
> I wanted to walk in with dignity and walk out the same way. I didn't want my daughter to be ashamed of what I was doing. God was gracious and kept me pretty straight and strong. I didn't think it would last much more than 30 seconds. I was going to say what I had to say, and I didn't care about what he had to say. The mediation ended up lasting five and one-half hours. We talked. I let him know the devastation he had created, why I was the only one there, that I would be at the execution, that he had done so much harm to so many people.
>
> When I walked out, I left everything with Jonathan and he was gracious enough to accept it. He accepted my forgiveness and he accepted responsibility for all of the pain he had caused my family. I knew by his words and actions that he was sincere. He did not deny that he had murdered Mitzi or the consequences of his actions. I saw life in his eyes that I had never seen before. He was more human than he had ever been before.
>
> Mediation gave me my first bit of peace. I could never accept what he did, but we came to terms with each other, and he knew definitely where I stood and I knew where he was. I didn't want to be friends with him or have casual conversation with him. That was not the purpose of the mediation. I had to reconcile myself to the fact that I was sitting down face to face with the man who had brutally murdered my daughter. I could never give him a stamp of approval or be his friend. But after this day I was

able to go on with my life, to think instead of being brain dead for the first time in 12 years. You cannot imagine what that feels like.

Paula's amazing experience vividly demonstrates one kind of reconciliation. She and Jonathan "came to terms" and in doing so set themselves free. Just coming to terms required almost superhuman courage and humanity on Paula's part, and it's probably more than most can imagine under similar circumstances. Other situations are easier and allow for different types of reconciliation. Just as relationships break apart in many ways, they also can be reconciled in many ways. Parents and children can listen to one another and decide to get along. Two people in the business world can resolve a dispute, agree to disagree, and continue to work together within certain ground rules. Divorced parents can put their problems behind them and act civilly in front of their children without being particularly good friends. Siblings can resolve their differences and become close again. Lovers with disagreements can become intimate. It all depends on who the two of you are, where you've been, and where you need to be.

Since reconciling is a choice and is not always possible, you have to decide whether or not to try to reconcile and also choose the type of reconciliation that makes sense in your case. You are an imperfect human and so is the person with whom you would like to reconcile. Sometimes the human frailties of the two of you prevent you from reconciling in any meaningful way, and continuing efforts to do so bring only frustration. Sometimes grievances are difficult enough, or the relationship unimportant enough, that you will choose to let sleeping dogs lie and terminate the relationship or simply hope the conflict will melt away over time. Often, however, too much is at stake to defer the matter or walk away, and you will conclude that you need to attempt reconciliation. The following sections offer some thoughts on creating an environment that helps with reconciliation, on deciding when to try, and on how to go about it.

Building an Environment for Reconciliation

You are the only person you can control, and trying to force your desires on another person most often leads, not to reconciliation, but to even further conflict, estrangement, and anger. If you try to meddle, advise, or criticize another, you will only run each of you to a frazzle and make both of your lives miserable. All you can do is control your own behavior and behave in a way that creates an environment where the other person will want to reconcile with you. Praying for the other person and your reconciliation, fostering trust between you, and behaving with humility will go a long way toward creating such an environment.

- Pray for those with whom you wish to reconcile and for the success of your endeavor. If we do not pray for others, even our enemies and those who persecute us, we continue to see only our own point of view. Prayer brings others into our hearts, helps us empathize, breaks down the hostility and distinction between them and us, and begins to make them into friends. Praying for God's help in your reconciliation will also help give you the courage to attempt what can be a difficult and risky endeavor. Bridges To Life victims often experience great apprehension, even fear, when they attend their first sessions with offenders. They fear the uncertainty and the vulnerability of sharing their intimate stories with people like those who hurt them. Offenders typically have similar fears. Nonetheless, they all gather up their courage and do it, and you may have to do the same in a difficult reconciliation situation. If you pray about your reconciliation, God will make it easier for you.

- Build trust, as lack of trust is probably the biggest problem for reconciliation. We create mistrust in many ways: by not being honest or not doing what we say we will do, by speaking out against another (particularly behind their back), by being angry, by failing to exhibit love. If we don't trust, we are wary of one another, are usually defensive, and build walls of suspicion. If something doesn't go to our liking, or someone seems to act unfairly, we assume the worst. We try to protect ourselves but end up only exposing our weakness, vulnerability, and bad side. To have true reconciliation, you have to develop true mutual trust. Trust is the unwritten and usually unspoken contract that allows people to believe in the honesty, integrity, reliability, and justice of one another. Trust has many dimensions, none more important than honesty. The most important thing you can do to foster mutual trust is to be honest, whether that term means being truthful in a general sense, doing what you say you will do, calling a spade a spade, being willing to confess and admit failure, being honest with yourself, or any of many other possibilities that you, no doubt, understand. True reconciliation requires complete honesty.

- Demonstrate humility rather than false pride or arrogance. Humility requires seeing yourself as you are, warts and all. It does not, however, allow self-recrimination—blaming or feeling sorry for yourself. If you allow self-recrimination, you have not reconciled with yourself. Laura Davis has noted in *I Thought We'd Never Speak Again*, "When we grow large enough to embrace our own faults and to honor the flawed humanity of another human being, we open the door to connection, integration, and love."[1] To reconcile, you need to be humble, not just in the sense of being gentle or meek, but also in the sense of being vulnerable and willing to be hurt. You have to be willing to go unnoticed, to be last, to receive the least.

After you have done your best to create an environment for reconciliation, you still face the question of whether or when you should go forward. The stage may or may not be set. Thus, you need to look closely at whether the time is right.

Deciding When to Seek Reconciliation

When should you seek reconciliation? Like so much here, that is a personal decision. The starting point is to look closely at yourself and your role in any conflict with another person. It's easy to blame the other person, but usually both people contribute to the situation and only you can control when you will seek to reconcile. Ask yourself questions such as:

- Has enough time passed since the conflict or estrangement that I can reflect carefully, objectively, and honestly on our relationship and look at the big picture?
- Why did the conflict happen? Who is responsible for what? Can I accept responsibility for my part?
- In what ways am I accountable to the other person? Can I acknowledge that accountability?
- Who do I want to be after reconciling?
- Have I repented and committed to change? If not, is long term reconciliation possible?
- Have I reconciled with myself?
- Have I reconciled with God concerning the situation?

Honestly answering such questions should tell you whether to try to reconcile with the other person. Without positive answers, your attempt to reconcile may appear to work at first but will probably lead to eventual frustration and further conflict.

However, when you understand your situation and are reconciled with yourself and God, you will know when to try to reconcile with another. God will tell you. Reconciling will nearly always work because you will be genuinely concerned about the other person as well as yourself and will approach the matter with an attitude of humility and grace.

Decide what kind of reconciliation—or what type of relationship—you want with the other person. Paula did not want a close relationship with Jonathan. She just wanted to come to terms with him. In your case, is just being able to communicate rationally and civilly enough, or do you need more? Do you want a business-like relationship, or do you want to be friends, or do you want to be lovers? In reaching this decision remember that reconciliation is a journey and not an event, and sometimes you may need to start small and allow your relationship to grow. First talk civilly, then become friends, then allow your relationship to grow as both of you think it should.

Let's assume you have done your homework and are ready to attempt to reconcile with someone. Since two people are required for reconciliation, you also have to consider the other person. Some level of conflict probably continues to exist and the other person may be highly emotional, filled with anger, bitterness, jealousy, sadness, or some other feeling that may make reconciliation difficult or impossible at the time. Do you suppose Paula could have come to terms with Jonathan on the day the trial was completed? Probably not. She needed more time to even consider it.

The other person's view of the situation between you is probably very different from yours, particularly if the two of you are from different cultures or generations or have other differences. Look carefully and objectively at the other person and figure out whether he is capable of reconciliation at the time. Is he still too angry or too hurt or too bitter to even consider reconciliation? Can he change as much as is needed for reconciliation to occur? Does the other person need more time to adjust to the situation and make reconciliation possible? You can always be surprised, but usually you won't be. If you listen, empathize, and care deeply about the other person's situation you can probably decide whether he is capable of reconciliation at the time.

Also consider the possibility of rejection and how you will react if your attempt at reconciliation falls on deaf ears. If you conclude the other person isn't ready or you could not handle rejection well, consider waiting. If you conclude both of you are ready to reconcile, and you can handle rejection if things don't work out, consider proceeding.

Seeking Reconciliation

When you have built a good environment and decided to seek reconciliation, how do you go about it? Using the right approach is absolutely essential. Whatever you do, put your past behind you and start from where you are. We discussed in Chapter 10 that we all can forgive but that forgetting often is not possible or even desirable. If you have hurt or been hurt by another, both of you will remember. This does not mean, however, that you have to beat up one another over what has already been done or try to fix what cannot be fixed. Decide the type of relationship you want from this day forward. Paula and Jonathan couldn't bring Mitzi back, but they could come to terms with what happened. Each reconciliation effort will be different and call for different actions. The following, however, are some guidelines that apply in most situations:

- Consider talking about talking. Make a contact and discuss with the other person whether reconciliation is possible and should even be discussed. You may find it helpful to send a letter proposing that you and the other person agree to try to agree. You agree to discuss your differences before you start to discuss them. Paula had an agreement to talk before talking with Jonathan.

- Don't take no too quickly. The other person must agree if you are to reconcile, but you may need to keep on pressing if you meet rejection at first. The other person may just need time to think and adjust to new possibilities. Think about the situation and judge the real meaning of a first rejection.

- Go slow. Surprisingly, you often need to go slow in order to move fast toward reconciliation. Both of you may need time to think about what is happening, adjust to changes, overlook some small issues, accept some disappointments. Taking your time, taking one small step at a time, may be necessary in a reconciliation journey in such situations.

- Try to engage in dialogue and tell and listen to your stories. Don't rehash the past as a way of casting blame, but discuss it as a way of understanding one another's humanity and preparing a path for the future.

- Listen with empathy. To reconcile, the two of you need to understand one another's needs, feelings, and emotions. Listening with empathy and walking in the other person's shoes will allow you to understand him and will encourage him to listen to you.

- Validate the other person. Acknowledge his humanity and value as a fellow human being. Regardless of the conflict, you can always find something positive to say. Say it.

- Address your own responsibility and accountability. If you have been wrong (and we are rarely perfect), confess and repent with a sincere apology. Honestly acknowledging your own mistakes is a sign of your strength and maturity and will set the stage for a candid discussion.

- Seek a win/win resolution. Most reconciliations involve differences where both people have interests that need to be addressed. Restoring the relationship as it was is not likely, and reconciliation is not likely to last or be productive if one person wins and the other loses. Instead, both people need to feel a sense of fairness, even if the issues between you are not always resolved. Reconciliation is about restoring relationships, not getting your way.

- Accept the other person as she is. Remember that you are trying to fix a relationship, not the other person. She may change, but if so, she has to change herself. You cannot do it for her.

- Remember that reconciliation isn't always possible, regardless of how much we work for it, hope for it, or pray for it. Reconciling takes two people, and sometimes two people just cannot get together. Be prepared to accept this possibility and move on with you life if necessary.

One final thought. Reconciliation doesn't always mean closure. Paula didn't feel her mediation with Jonathan attained closure. She says, "Closure—there is no such animal. That is a media word, not a victim word. There is never closure. How do you close burying your child? You don't. Neither my mediation nor Jonathan's execution gave me closure. There is no such word for victims. One chapter ended and another started, and I gained a little more peace. But I don't have closure."

Similarly, reconciliation may not bring closure for you in many situations. It can, however, bring you and the other person more peace and start a better chapter in your relationship, and that makes it worth the effort.

STUDY QUESTIONS

1. Why did Paula feel such a need to reconcile with Johathan?
2. Can you reconcile with someone else without first reconciling with yourself and with God? If no, why not?
3. How do you know when you have developed a friendship with God?
4. List several people who have affected your life (such as your parents, siblings, or friends) and the types of relationships that you would like to have with each of them.
5. Review chapters 6 through 10—responsibility, accountability, confession, repentance, and forgiveness. How does each step build toward reconciliation?
6. What role does trust play in reconciliation?
7. What are the most important considerations in deciding when reconciliation with someone is possible and when you should try to reconcile?

12

RESTITUTION

"How can I make amends when I don't even know all those I've hurt?"
Inmate, Hamilton Unit

B ob and Kathy Connell live on their ranch just outside Crockett, Texas. Around midnight on a cool October night a few years ago, four of their children—Allen, Laurel, Lee, and Sara Jo—were driving home from a church party in Centerville, Texas, following a Friday night high-school football game. About seven miles from home, a local man, impaired with alcohol and drugs, crashed into their car head-on at seventy miles per hour and murdered them all. Kathy and Bob received that most feared of all phone calls just after midnight. Let me tell you about their four children who were killed, in Kathy's words from the victim impact statement used in connection with the conviction and sentencing of their killer.

> James Allen Connell was 19 years old with an 18 year old wife and two month old baby. He loved his family more than life, and was more of a man at 19 than most are at 30. Allen had a dry wit that would leave you laughing and a tenderness with his wife and baby that would make you cry. He was 6'2" with a 29 inch waist. He would find the craziest shirt in the closet and the rattiest hat on the rack to rope in. Other than time with his family, he was happiest on horseback at a rodeo or roping, or hitting golf balls in the pasture behind his house. Now his son gets to

learn about his daddy by the hundreds of questions about the man in the picture on his wall.

Laurel Leanne Connell, Lauri-Darlin she was called by family and friends, was 17 years old, waist length hair, a senior in high school, honor student, homecoming queen nominee, District FFA officer, rode on two ranch rodeo teams, the Sr. Girls AND the Sr. Boys. She was a rodeo queen contestant as well, and beautiful by anybody's standards. She was going to Texas A&M the following fall, to begin her studies to prepare for vet school, something she had worked very hard to accomplish. But these were not her greatest accomplishments. Laurel taught me more about how to treat people than anyone else in my life. She was always looking for the good in everyone.

Thomas Lee Connell was 14 years old, already 5'10" and 170 pounds. Lee was the baby I knew before he came, knew he was a boy, knew he was red headed. He was the person we all hope to have in our lives. He liked the same old rock and roll music and same old classic Mustangs as I did, and could finish my sentences for me most of the time. Lee said he either wanted to be a lawyer or a preacher, he wasn't sure yet, and we always told him he had both ends of the spectrum covered. He had an amazing sense of humor, and a mischievousness about him that was endearing to everyone. He never met a stranger, and it didn't matter what you looked like, how old you were, your socioeconomic status or your race, he had time to get to know you and made the effort.

Sara Jo, the baby of the group, was 12 going on 16. She wanted to be 16 from the time she arrived, and was already anticipating a car, makeup, prom dresses, and dating. Her daddy's "Honey Baby." She had long blonde hair, the kind most people get from a bottle, and beautiful skin that glowed. She was the nurturer of the bunch, she loved babies and children, and animals as well. Sara planned to go to medical school to be a pediatrician.

It all ended on that sad October night. John, a good ol' boy from the same small community, had too many beers and prescription drugs without a prescription and tried to straighten a curve on a farm-to-market road at seventy miles per hour. He hit them head on with his large pick-up truck and murdered them all.

Laurel's small Toyota Tercel—the one Bob had bought her to take to Texas A&M—never had a chance. It was crushed and mangled beyond recognition.

Again, in Kathy's words: "Laurel's face was gone. She and Lee were so bad they had to sprinkle them with some formaldehyde powder and zip them up in a body bag and we never saw them again. The left side of Allen's face was almost gone, and lots or reconstruction work had to happen for the funeral and for his wife's sake. Sara did not have any visible external injuries. She just looked like Sleeping Beauty that would never wake up."

Can you even imagine Bob and Kathy's pain and sorrow? Twenty-four pallbearers, so many people to notify and talk to, four death certificates, four tombstones, everything they had done and dreamed of wiped out in a split second. They got a life sentence. But what was right for John? What should Bob and Kathy demand of and for him, and what should he do as a result of murdering— admittedly without malice—Allen and Laurel and Lee and Sara Jo? These questions raise the subject of restitution.

Restitution is what you actually do to make amends or pay back another for a harm that you have done. Restitution means, to the extent possible, giving back or "making right" that which you have wronged within the victim's physical, emotional, spiritual, financial, and social being. It usually is voluntary and relates to restoring justice and fair treatment. When we harm another person, we in some way take or withhold something that is rightfully theirs. The drunk driver took the Connell's children, and Bridges To Life offenders have taken money, possessions, or peace of mind from their victims. You may have taken your parent's peace of mind by rebelling against them, or your spouse's freedom by exercising too much control, or your partner's profits in a business deal, or done any of many other actions that violated a social contract between you and another and caused her pain. Or similar things may have happened to you. If such things happened, justice and fair treatment say that the offender make amends by, insofar as possible, returning what has been taken. When an offender is fair and tries to reduce the hurt or make the other person whole, he is making restitution.

Restitution is the "proof of the pudding." It's the action that demonstrates that you really have accepted responsibility, acknowledged accountability, and decided to do something about your offense of another. When you make restitution you do what you can to be fair with those to whom you are accountable. An offender at the Kyle unit explained it this way: "I've really done some bad things. In the future, I will be an asset to my city, state, country, and society. I will be a good father to my daughter." If he does what he promised, he will make restitution.

In his famous satire, *The Screwtape Letters,* theologian C. S. Lewis explained the need for such action by having the devil tell a young demon who is about to lose someone to virtue and true Christianity (the devil's enemy):

> It remains to consider how we can retrieve this disaster. The great thing is to prevent his doing anything. As long as he does not convert it into action, it does not matter how much he thinks about this new repentance. Let the little brute wallow in it. Let him, if he has any bent that way, write a book about it; that is often an excellent way of sterilising the seeds which the Enemy plants in a human soul. Let him do anything but act. No amount of piety in his imagination and affections will harm us if we can keep it out of his will. As one of the humans has said, active habits are strengthened by repetition but passive ones are weakened. The more often he feels without acting, the less he will be able ever to act, and, in the long run, the less he will be able to feel. [1]

Thus, restitution normally is an action that follows true repentance. Another way to look at restitution is to consider it an effort to reduce the "net" hurt. Businesses consider their net profits or losses as the total profit minus certain expenses. Similarly, an offender can cause a smaller net hurt by providing restitution—it is a help that subtracts from the total hurt the offender has imposed on a victim.

Let's look now at what restitution is not. Restitution is not vengeance, revenge, retribution, or retaliation. When you seek any of these you seek to respond to a wrong with another wrong: you try to fix one hurt by imposing another hurt, reduce pain by imposing pain.

Restitution is not punishment, or the forceful infliction of suffering. Some feel that criminal penalties—fines, jail or prison time, even the death penalty—are forms of restitution. Punishment is often appropriate and may have either of two functions. One is to look backward and seek to impose on an offender the level of suffering he deserves for the offense he committed. The other is to look to the future and try to prevent the same offense again by removing the offender from society or motivating him to avoid behaving that way again. Both functions serve society, but they do not pay off a "debt to society." An offender spending time in a juvenile facility or prison is not paying restitution. Doing so may discharge a debt imposed by the system, but it does nothing to restore fairness and justice to the victim of the offender's action.

Two examples illustrate what restitution is. First is the story Jesus told in Luke 19. The Romans had levied heavy taxes against all under their control. The Jews opposed these taxes but were still forced to pay, so the tax collectors, who often made themselves rich by gouging their fellow Jews, were among the most unpopular people in Israel. Zacchaeus was one of the hated tax collectors. In spite of this, Jesus went home with him and loved him, and Zacchaeus repented. When he did, he stood before the Lord and said, "Sir, from now on I will give half my wealth to the poor, and if I find I have overcharged anyone on his taxes, I will penalize myself by giving him back four times as much!"

By giving to the poor and making restitution to those he had cheated, Zacchaeus showed internal change by outward action. Jesus responded by telling him, "This shows that salvation has come to this home today."

The second example of restitution is the story of how Bob and Cathy handled the terrible aftermath of the loss of their four children. They worked closely with the District Attorney and

Attorney General's office handling the case, and their views were important in the decision as to what should happen to the drunk driver who killed their children. They could have recommended a very long prison sentence for the offender—one that would have precedent in similar cases and would have thrown away the key to John's cell door.

Bob and Cathy prayed and thought deeply about the matter and considered all the relevant circumstances. They were able to subdue the unending pain long enough to remember that, as bad as his actions were, John had no malice in the murder of their children and was deeply remorseful. They also considered that he had four young children to support, and his going to prison would mean four innocent children would lose their father while they were growing up. Thus, they opted for restitution rather than retribution, revenge, or vengeance. They knew, of course, that John could not take back what he had done. He could not return their children. He could, however, ever so slightly, reduce their net hurt by contributing to society in ways that help reduce the chances of the same thing happening to other children and other parents. As a result, John was sentenced to only 180 days in jail, but was required to provide a form of restitution for ten years. This included:

- Accepting a ten year probated sentence
- Attending AA meetings regularly
- Maintaining four crosses at the location of the wreck
- Carrying pictures of the children he killed in his wallet
- Doing public service work at the high school the children had attended
- Making anti-drunk driving presentations to various groups as requested by the Connells

While these actions were required of John rather than voluntary on his part, they are examples of the spirit of Christian restitution. They were intended to have the offender do what he could to make amends to his victims and society for his actions.

Restitution can be viewed from two perspectives: from the perspective of a victim who may expect or ask for it and from the perspective of an offender who needs to offer it. Let's discuss both perspectives.

RESTITUTION FROM A VICTIM'S PERSPECTIVE

It happened in April, during a freak spring norther and snowstorm in the Texas Panhandle. Jesse Doiron was driving a Dodge van from Albuquerque to Chicago, delivering a load of training materials and student belongings to another of his employer's training sites. After a long morning of fighting black ice and increasingly large snow drifts, and occasionally helping extract ditched travelers, Jesse pulled into a service station for gasoline and a brief rest.

Two scruffy looking men with a big, furry, mixed-breed dog named Bear were also at the station. They told Jesse their car had broken down and asked if they could ride with him on his drive north. Jesse was somewhat reluctant—his van was loaded and the situation didn't feel quite right—but he agreed to squeeze them in and they hit the road. That night Jesse got a room and the other two shared one at a small roadside motel. The next morning they proceeded on their journey. Jesse, still with the uneasy feeling, considered just leaving them but decided not to, mainly for the sake of the dog.

Mid-morning, on an isolated stretch of road just north of Pampa, Texas, one of the men demanded, "Pull over. I need to take a leak." Jesse stopped, one of the men slid the van door open, and they both got out and walked to the rear, out of Jesse's sight. Jesse's next memory is of being hit repeatedly with a three-pound shop hammer—of feeling no pain but believing for sure he was going to die—of being kicked with hard, well-worn boots—of trying to jump out of the van but being restrained by his seat belt—of being pulled and pushed—of understanding his own mortality—of finally jumping out of his moving van—of the van running over his feet—of being buried in a deep snow drift, looking up through the mist as he heard the van drive away.

Jesse heard the van return before he could garner the strength to raise his head or move. He assumed they were returning to be sure he was dead. They had just returned to get their dog. He heard them calling Bear, heard Bear run by, heard the van drive away again. For a long time no one stopped to help him, but Jesse was eventually able, by sheer willpower, to get up, struggle to the main road, and flag down a highway department snowplow, which took him to a hospital in Pampa. He had multiple injuries from the beating—concussion and cuts, a collapsed left lung, several broken ribs, a separated shoulder, cuts running from his feet to his face. During emergency exploratory surgery, doctors found that his spleen was detached and were able to reconnect it.

His tormentors were captured within two weeks and were ultimately convicted of attempted capital murder. One confessed and received fifteen years in prison and the other received thirty years. But the convictions gave Jesse no peace.

Seven years later, Jesse was working a stint in Saudi Arabia, still wrestling with the severe beating and trying to come to grips with himself, those who assaulted him, and their actions. He says, "An acquaintance called me up one day and said, 'There's going to be a public execution tomorrow, do you want to go?' I said, 'Heck yes, I'd like to go', wishing it could be my former tormentors I would witness facing a guillotine. The next day I witnessed three men beheaded with a sword. It was held on the vast asphalt parking lot of the Central Mosque in Riyadh, within the front ranks of a rowdy, circus-like crowd that included 1500 men, women, and children."

Jesse felt the beheading was a slimy, greasy affair, and that even his witnessing it was somehow wrong. It detracted from his sense of dignity, and imagining his former tormentors giving their lives in such a way was no help at all. However, watching the circus-like atmosphere of the beheading did help him realize an essential truth about restitution from a victim's point of view: receiving restitution without forgiving the offender is really retribution. It may replace some or all of what was taken, but it doesn't bring peace to the heart and soul. Jesse observed, "I realized that nothing is going away. Whatever happened, happened, and nothing can erase it and seeing someone else suffer or even having an offender try to pay back won't make you feel any better. True peace can only come from inside you: from you granting forgiveness to the offender and not from receiving restitution from him."

Receiving restitution from an offender who has hurt you can sometimes help. If someone steals your car, having it returned provides you with transportation. If someone steals your money, you are justified in wanting it returned to help you in your daily life. At other times, however, an offender simply cannot make the restitution you want and cannot return what he has taken from you. Those who assaulted Jesse cannot restore his sense of well-being, and certainly John cannot return the Connells' four children. But regardless of whether or not what is lost can be restored, restitution alone brings little peace.

Depending on restitution to solve your problem or make you whole is like depending on confession or repentance from an offender. Doing so places your healing in the hands of someone you cannot control, and every time restitution fails to occur you are victimized again. Better to have your healing governed by what you can control—your own feelings and actions.

Even when it occurs, receiving restitution alone is not likely to bring the internal change of heart that is necessary for true healing, because restitution usually involves things rather than feelings, the past rather than the present or future. True healing comes from within you, and the key seems to be to search your heart and find a way to love and forgive rather than to depend on an offender offering restitution. The book of Leviticus provided the Hebrews a guide for such an approach. In Chapter 19:19, Moses told his people, "Don't seek vengeance. Don't bear a grudge; but love your neighbor as yourself..."

Jesus took Moses' principle an important step further in Matthew 5: 43-47, and extended the idea of love to our enemies—presumably including those who have hurt us:

> There is a saying, "Love your friends and hate your
> enemies." But I say: Love your enemies! Pray for those
> who persecute you! In that way you will be acting as true

sons of your Father in heaven. For he gives his sunlight to both the evil and the good, and sends rain on the just and on the unjust too. If you love only those who love you, what good is that? Even scoundrels do that much. If you are friendly only to your friends, how are you different from anyone else? Even the heathen do that.

What can we learn from Jesse, the Connells, and the Bible about expecting or demanding restitution? Several things can be summarized as follows:

- Each situation needs to be considered on a case-by-case basis. In a criminal setting, the concepts of restitution and penal justice should be kept separate, with violators dealt with as appropriate in the best interest of society at large. Justice dictated long prison sentences for the men who nearly killed Jesse, and concepts of restitution do not change that.

- Perfect restitution is not always possible. The past cannot be returned, and when you depend on restitution for healing you turn control of your own healing over to someone else.

- Forgiveness is necessary if restitution is to heal. Think of Jesse's conclusion after watching the beheadings. His forgiving, not some idea of restitution, is what gave him some peace.

- Love, not vengeance, needs to drive your expectation for restitution. Think of how the Connells' requests for restitution addressed the needs of John's children and of the broader society rather than their own.

- Accepting an act of restitution as a sincere token of an offender's remorse and repentance can help both offender and victim progress along their healing journey.

Thus, receiving restitution that is demanded or expected from an offender has little healing value, while receiving that which is freely offered as a confirmation of the offender's accountability, remorse, and repentance can work wonders. Now let's discuss true restitution from an offender's perspective.

RESTITUTION FROM AN OFFENDER'S PERSPECTIVE

Bridges To Life offenders are encouraged to make restitution for their offenses. Doing so is a natural consequence of the preceding steps of the Bridges To Life process:

- If you accepted responsibility for hurting someone, fairness dictates that you make restitution to reduce the net effect and minimize the extent of your responsibility.
- If you acknowledged accountability, you know who to make restitution to.
- When you truly repent, restitution will naturally follow. On the other hand, claims of confessing offenses and committing to change through repentance are nothing more than pious frauds—jailhouse religion—if you don't follow through and try to make things right with restitution.
- How can you expect continuing forgiveness from another person or long-lasting reconciliation unless you do what you can to fairly reduce the net hurt to the one you offended?

Several of these steps in the healing process—particularly confessing, forgiving, and reconciling—involve dealing with yourself, God, and another. Similarly, restitution has all three aspects.

Making Restitution to Yourself

When we think of making restitution to ourselves, our first thought is usually to reward ourselves: to go on a shopping spree, or take the afternoon off school or work, or just have a favorite ice cream cone. Restitution is not a reward, however, and such superficial actions, while appropriate under many circumstances, are temporary at best and don't heal our hurt in any meaningful way.

So how do you make restitution to yourself? Let's start by reviewing what restitution is. It's what you do to make amends for harm you've done and try to make one whole again. Therefore, let's explore what you can do to foster your own wholeness.

When you are whole, you are fully human and you behave as humans are expected to behave. You have relationships with relatives and friends. You have a rich spiritual life. You love. You have hope. You see and understand beauty. You are thankful. You feel empathy and compassion. You forgive and don't hold grudges. You aren't oppressed by shame or unfounded guilt. Add your own elements that are necessary for a full life for you. What does your complete list look like? It follows, of course, that if your life is missing anything on the list, you are not completely whole. Making restitution to yourself means addressing one or more of the missing elements in your life and moving—at least a little bit— toward your own wholeness.

Consider several Bridges To Life offenders discussed in previous chapters and how each was able to move toward wholeness and in doing so make restitution to himself.

- Mavis (Chapter 6) recognized she wasn't responsible for her baby's death and moved beyond her guilt and shame.
- Lornita (Chapter 8) confessed to her father and restored her relationship with him.
- Danny (Chapter 9) listened to Kathy Connell describe the loss of her four children and learned to be empathetic.
- Ronnie (Chapter 10) accepted God's forgiveness, forgave himself, and got his humanity back.

Think about how these individuals added missing elements to their lives. Each person did her own thing in her own way, but all followed one or more of the Bridges To Life principles. They looked to God for help and guidance and told their stories to empathetic listeners. They accepted responsibility for their behavior and acknowledged their accountability. They confessed, repented, forgave, and reconciled to the extent and in the way that was appropriate for them. In doing so, they became more fully human and made restitution to themselves.

You can do the same things. Taking one of the Bridges To Life steps discussed in a preceding chapter moves you a small step toward becoming whole. If you take one of them, you are making restitution to yourself. The more steps you take, the more fully you make restitution.

Making Restitution to God

We sin against God when we hurt or offend our fellow man, and only God can tell us how to make restitution to Him for our actions. His word tells us that we make restitution to Him when we make restitution to those we have hurt or offended. Leviticus 6: 2-5 makes this point:

> And the Lord said to Moses, "If anyone sins against me by refusing to return a deposit on something borrowed or rented, or by refusing to return something entrusted to him, or by robbery, or by oppressing his neighbor, or by finding a lost article and lying about it, swearing that he doesn't have it—on the day he is found guilty of any such sin, he shall restore what he took, adding a twenty percent fine, and give it to the one he has harmed, and on the same day he shall bring his guilt offering to the Tabernacle."

Similarly, Matthew 25: 37-40 tells us how love for others is love for God:

> Then these righteous ones will reply, "Sir, when did we ever see you hungry and feed you? Or thirsty and give you anything to drink? Or a stranger, and help you? Or naked, and clothe you? When did we ever see you sick or in prison, and visit you?"
> And I, the King, will tell them, "When you did it to these my brothers you were doing it to me!"

Thus, we show our care for God through our care for others: for the small people of the world, the needy, the poor, those who cannot return our care and concern, and those we have offended and hurt. When we care for others, we make restitution to God.

Making Restitution to Others

Restitution to others is important—it's the basis of making restitution to ourselves and to God—and we must do it correctly. But what does that mean? When? To whom? How should we make amends for what we have done? Each person will have to decide, and each individual situation will require something different. The Bridges To Life process will provide you guidance.

Earlier in the chapter we discussed how the steps of the Bridges To Life process logically and naturally lead to restitution. Let's look now at how the same steps will answer some of your questions and guide you forward.

- Accepting responsibility tells you when and for what you need to make restitution. If you conclude you are the cause of pain or loss to another, then you are responsible for doing something to amend it. Richard (Chapter 6) finally accepted responsibility for committing burglaries. He should also make amends for them.

- Acknowledging accountability tells you whom you should make restitution to. You make it to those to whom you are accountable. Lawrence (Chapter 7) murdered his best friend. He's accountable to his friend's mother and should make restitution to her. Others are accountable to friends, relatives, and society at large.

- Your confession guides you in making restitution. It reminds you of the specifics of your offense and helps you make your restitution respond to what you've done. Doing good things for another may be helpful, but such actions do not have the power of restitution unless they directly respond to the hurt you caused. Making amends for the specifics you mentioned in your confession will keep you on track, and offering restitution with the same humility, respect, and emotion contained in your confession will make your amends more acceptable to the other person. Lornita (Chapter 8) was specific in her confession to her father. Making amends for those specifics will make her restitution relevant.

- Your repentance reinforces the purpose of your restitution: it helps insure that your focus will be on the one you hurt and not on yourself. The empathy that Danny (Chapter 9) learned from his encounter with Kathy helps him focus his restitution on other victims of drunk drivers.

- Forgiveness helps your offer of restitution to be acceptable. If a person has forgiven you, he will probably accept your offer of restitution with grace and love. Jack's wife (Chapter 10) will be better able to accept his restitution because Jack asked for forgiveness and she forgave him.

- Reconciliation establishes a relationship with the person you have hurt that allows restitution to happen. It's hard or impossible to make amends to someone with whom you have no relationship. Jonathan (Chapter 11) couldn't make amends to Paula for killing her daughter because he was sentenced to death and was executed. Under different circumstances, however, their having come to terms with one another could have made possible attempts at restitution more likely to be acceptable.

Jason Heffner's story is one of contrasts: extreme crime and admirable restitution. He credits God and Bridges To Life for guiding his journey. Jason was the son of a troubled home— neglect, abuse, addiction, all circumstances so typical in the lives of Bridges To Life offenders. He started drinking at age seven and never finished high school. He became a heavy drug user and assaulted, terrorized, and otherwise victimized many people. He was convicted of felony drug possession, felony flight to avoid prosecution, and conspiracy to commit capital murder against a public official. Jason spent a year in a high security prison in Arizona and eleven years, four months, twenty-nine days in Texas prisons, where he became a major gang leader and continued using drugs. He was denied parole four times because of disciplinary infractions. Jason was, to say the least, a bad dude.

Jason joined Bridges To Life without really knowing what it was. He now says about this experience:

> I thought I was doing these things to survive. Bridges To Life taught me for the first time that I was hurting people and didn't have a right to do these things to people. When Connie Hilton told the story of her husband's murder and her rape and near murder, I rationalized and justified the actions of those who did it. See, I always felt sorry for myself. I thought I was the victim. I had to learn to face me, Jason Heffner. I had to talk to Jason and ask him some questions and I didn't like what I heard. I was afraid to take responsibility. The pain in the eyes of Connie and others showed me how much I was responsible for and I learned how to receive forgiveness. It completely turned everything around for me. Were it not for God getting through to me through the Bridges To Life program, then I would be on death row today. You see, a punk I know raped a girl whose mother I'm close to. Before, I would have killed him. Instead, I turned him in and the officials took care of him.

Jason has been out of prison for several years and is leading a life filled with amazing acts of restitution. He is remaining clean and sober. He is married and owns his own house. He works as an automotive technician and is a fire fighter with the county fire and rescue department, where he has saved the lives of several accident victims. He carries a badge and works with law enforcement, frequently driving police cars and helping make arrests. He speaks to high school students about prisons and victimizing people. He is a father, a companion, a man. He understands he can't return things to the way they were, but he can certainly make restitution for what he has done. He says, "I sit in awe sometimes. God sees the change in me, and he's going to use me to get through to someone else. Tell them Jason loves Jesus."

What can we learn about restitution from Jason's story? Several things.

- You cannot always make full restitution or make all your victims whole. Jason could never make amends to all the victims of his criminal activity.

- You can always do your best, even if that is limited to avoiding the same or similar trouble in the future. Society probably would have been happy with Jason if his only restitution had been to avoid criminal activity after his release.

- Restitution requires action. Thinking about it, planning it, or talking about it does nothing. You have to do something.

- Your restitution needs to respond to your offense. Jason's teaching high school students about crime and prison relates directly to his offense.

- You can make restitution even if your victim is not aware of it. Few of Jason's victims are aware of what he is doing.

A final thought: Even though your motive may be to help another, the primary beneficiary of your actions when you make restitution to another is you. Jason's main message was how good his actions made him feel and how caring about others was healing him. It will be the same for you.

STUDY QUESTIONS

1. Describe the difference between serving a prison sentence or paying a fine and making restitution.
2. What happens when I expect restitution from someone but never get it?
3. How do I make restitution to myself?
4. How do I make restitution to God?
5. How can you make restitution if you are incarcerated?

6. Describe an occasion when someone surprised you with kindness.

7. List some specific things you can do to make amends or pay back for some hurt you have caused.

13

THE JOURNEY

"It will give me important tools to use but only God and myself can truly be responsible for my life."
Inmate, LeBlanc Unit

Reflect, if you will, on those Bridges To Life participants mentioned in this book. The offenders have, for the most part, behaved badly and been criminals for most of their lives. Recall Richard, from Chapter 6, who was neglected and abused from birth and then moved on to drugs, shoplifting, and burglary. Or Lornita, from Chapter 8, who grew up in a stable home but nevertheless went astray at a young age. Remember all the others who have been involved with bad behavior or crime for a lifetime. A miraculous, quick resolution of their problems and conflicts was not likely. And most of the victim volunteers suffered tragedy and pain of the very worst sort—the type that people never get over and usually spend years just learning to deal with.

Similarly, you cannot reasonably expect to end the fourteen-week Bridges To Life experience with all your problems solved, totally at peace with yourself and others. The most you can expect is to be better equipped for a long journey and to have taken a few steps in the right direction.

Most problems and conflicts are like a hurricane that starts as an area of low pressure and slowly swirling winds far out in the ocean, becomes larger and stronger as it moves toward land, and develops into a fearful, destructive force when it hits the shore.

Similarly, most of the problems we face started small, grew over time, and have become complex, messy affairs that are difficult to resolve. Just as they didn't occur overnight, they cannot be resolved overnight or by participating in one Bridges To Life experience or by reading one book, even *Restoring Peace*! Solving difficult problems and conflicts and restoring peace in our lives require a journey.

The journey is not easy or straightforward. Two examples illustrate what the journey of peace and reconciliation is not and is.

Passage through the Panama Canal demonstrates what your journey of peace is not. Think about going through the Canal. Your only option is where you start—from the Atlantic or the Pacific Ocean. Once you establish your starting point, your destination is always the opposite end. The journey is always the same for everyone who takes it. You go through the same sets of locks, over the same lake, through the same cuts, always in the same order. All trips take approximately equal time and everyone arrives at the same place. Such a predictable, straightforward process works—is essential—for a journey through a canal, but it doesn't work at all for a journey of peace and reconciliation.

Now think of a shopper's journey through a department store. She is single-minded and shops her own way as best fits her needs. She starts at the store entrance, and after that the trip is up to her. She starts and stops. She looks, tries on a garment, thinks about buying, decides it doesn't fit or doesn't look just right. She asks questions, gets opinions, goes back into the dressing room, and tries on something else. Our shopper buys some items, rejects others, and keeps on moving. Next season she returns to do it all over again!

Your journey toward peace will be much like the shopper's trip. You will need to start from where you are, but after that nothing is predictable. Both your goal and your process should be your own. The Bridges To Life experience is in the order that seems to be logical for most people and situations. Each individual, however, needs to approach the healing process much like the shopper does her task: explore, think, test, adopt, reject, and most importantly, expect to go through various parts of the process again and again. Problems that developed over a long time usually require a long time to solve, and sometimes they don't stay solved and have to be addressed several times.

Your journey will not be easy or without risk. Acknowledging your responsibility and accountability requires a self-knowledge that is difficult to achieve and that can plunge you into a downward cycle of guilt and shame. Confessing and forgiving often require superhuman effort, more guts than you ever felt you had. Repentance requires change to a new life, with all its scary unknowns and reasons to just let your life stay as it is. Being forgiven and reconciling require another person, whom you cannot control, to act as you would like them to. Thus, you must know when you start that you will be traveling on a risky journey— somewhat less risky because you are supported by a loving God, but risky just the same.

Restoring Peace has given you tools to use to bring peace into your life, but what you do with them is your decision. You face a journey that only you can travel. As you begin your journey, remember several important things.

- There is much good in you and you need to congratulate yourself for making the effort to improve yourself and your relationships. Remember the good and allow it to win out over bad behavior or other problems you are facing.

- Your inherent sense of what is right and wrong and the Bible's great moral codes will help you set your destination. Rely on them.

- The Bridges To Life process, based on biblical principles of responsibility, accountability, confession, repentance, forgiveness, reconciliation, and restitution, will provide a road map for your journey. Review the preceding chapters of *Restoring Peace* as often as necessary to stay on track.

- You are not traveling alone. God loves you, will make the journey with you, and will carry you when you need to be carried.

- God gives you hope—a realistic dream for a better future—when you put your life in His hands.
- You and God working together can attain that better future.

The important thing is for you to take the journey. Tom Ferris' tragic story demonstrates the pain and suffering you will feel if you cannot or are not willing to proceed. Tom is a businessman from Katy, Texas. He grew up in an upper middle class family, with an older brother and two sisters. He and his brother, Rob, were close—playmates, competitors, teammates, best friends. When Rob was seventeen he attended a concert with his girlfriend. After the concert a gang of young men followed them, raped Rob's girlfriend, stabbed him several times, and left them by the side of the road to die. They both lived, but Rob was never able to get over the trauma, and he was not able to deal effectively with many of the problems he faced. Over the years, Tom and Rob maintained a relationship, but it was never as close as it had been or as Tom hoped it would be.

During the Thanksgiving holiday several years ago Tom took his wife and two children to Big Bend. While there, he checked his answering machine and heard a message from Rob asking him to go hunting in east Texas. Tom erased the tape, not knowing that was the last time he would ever hear his brother's voice. When Tom called his brother's home, he got no answer. Tom called again and again and got no answer until Rob's roommate, Ken, (an older man whom Rob had allowed to move in with him) finally answered. Rob was missing. The next few months were a blur for Tom: conflicting stories from Ken, bad and good police investigations, searching the bars and haunts that Rob frequented, combing Rob's property with cadaver dogs, finding Rob's truck but not Rob, evidence that Rob had been murdered in his own home by Ken, and, finally, Ken disappearing,

Ken's flight was advertised on *America's Most Wanted* and as a result he was located in Oklahoma and arrested. He confessed to murdering Rob—to shooting him through the head with Rob's 270-caliber deer rifle after an argument over a small amount of money. Ken was sentenced to thirty-five years in prison, probably a life sentence because of his age. He claimed, however, and claims to this day, that he does not know where Rob's body is located. Ken says he hired a couple of Banditos gang members to take care of the details.

Tom continues to search for his brother's body, just as the nightmares about what happened continue. Tom and his sisters erected a tombstone next to those of their mother and father, but there is no grave. Tom has tried to arrange a Victim Offender Mediation Dialogue session (similar to the one Paula participated in—Chapter 11) with Ken, but Ken refuses to participate. Ken refuses to take a journey toward peace, and, therefore, Tom is unable to pursue effectively many parts of his. Think of the effect on both of them.

Tom has to deal with the unspeakable horror of losing his brother to a violent death at the hands of someone who claimed to be his friend. But he cannot really heal. He cannot find his brother's body and he believes that Ken is refusing to come clean, and Ken will not communicate with him. Ken does not demonstrate accountability, nor genuinely confess, nor repent. There is no hint of reconciliation or restitution. Ken made one statement at the trial: "I just wanna go fishin." Tom feels re-victimized each day. He works at forgiving but the walls of resistance refuse to fall away. His family is also suffering, but they are unable to discuss the situation. Tom's pain and hurt feel almost as fresh as they did when Rob first disappeared.

And think about Ken. While it's hard to sympathize with him, he is a human being too, and there must be at least some small corner of his soul that is wounded and unable to heal and be at peace. How can his wound heal if he refuses to confront his crime? Will he die in prison, a bitter, sad old man who refused to make an effort?

Think about how a journey toward peace and reconciliation could help both Tom and Ken, if only they could take it. Think about your own situation and take the journey if it needs to be taken. Unlike Tom, you probably have a choice.

What does your destination look like and what do you hope for? Each person will have a different journey. Consider the words of Debra Collins, a Bridges To Life graduate:

> Hope in a very dark place.
> Love in a place where hurt, anger, shame and humiliation are the rulers.
> Kindness where rudeness and ugliness live.
> Morality where immorality is stored.
> Remembrance where most have been forgotten.
> A time of love and understanding to those who have never known such.
> The freedom to be who I was intended to be.

Debra described the essence of Bridges To Life. Our hope and prayer is that she also described your journey of peace and reconciliation.

STUDY QUESTIONS

1. What are the most important things you can learn about your journey into the future from this chapter?
2. What have you discovered during the last twelve chapters that is most important to you?
3. List some of your good characteristics that you can build on in a journey of peace with someone you have hurt.
4. Review the process of responsibility, accountability, confession, repentance, forgiveness, reconciliation and restitution. Which of these steps do you need to concentrate on first in your journey to restore peace?
5. What happens to us if we refuse to take a journey of peace and reconciliation that needs to be taken?

Appendix A

BRIDGES TO LIFE HIGHLIGHTS

Since 2000, Bridges To Life has completed 434 projects in 41 Texas prisons and as of 2013 is operating in 30 prisons throughout the state of Texas plus several juvenile and transitional facilities. The Bridges To Life curriculum has also been used in 10 states and three foreign countries.

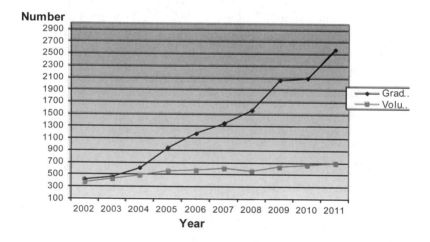

As illustrated in the chart above, significant growth in offender participation over the years has been possible even with the same number of volunteers. The phasing in of a revised curriculum, which includes this *Restoring Peace* book, requires offender participants do more homework outside of group meeting times. This has significantly improved the ratio of offenders to volunteers in each project, resulting in increased efficiency in program delivery as well as the ability to reach more offenders every year.

BTL could not provide services without the generous donation of volunteer time. Community support includes thousands of hours donated by volunteer facilitators and victim volunteers, and facilities to conduct the projects in correctional units throughout Texas. In 2012, our volunteers contributed more than 34,000 volunteer hours, representing an "in-kind" value of more than $700,000. The volunteers are absolutely essential to fulfilling the mission and goals of the program.

RECIDIVISM

The latest completed sample of BTL graduates for 3 year recidivism rates is very encouraging. The large, diversified sample group **includes 1,283 inmates who participated in BTL in 17 different prisons and were released from 2005 to 2008**. The **recidivism rate for this group is 18.16%** and is broken out into:

- Offenders returning for committing new crimes—15.36% (197)
- Offenders returning for technical violations of parole— 2.8% (36)
- Offenders returning to prison for committing a violent crime—2.0% (26)

Nationwide, these rates are reported to have remained "largely stable since the mid-1990's," varying between 38% and 40%. (Pew Center State of Recidivism Study 2011). **A subset of the above BTL study includes 558 inmates released from 12 various TDCJ Institutional Division (ID) Units, long term prisons that house more violent offenders. We are pleased to report that the recidivism rate for this group is 14.7%, with only 1.3% returning for a violent crime.** This is in comparison with Texas reports that inmates released in 2005 and 2006 from ID prisons had a recidivism rate of 26 to 27% (Texas Legislative Board Report 2009 and 2011). BTL is one of the programs that has contributed to a decrease in recidivism in Texas, and BTL graduates still show a significantly lower recidivism rate than the average for the nation and for Texas.

RECOGNITION

- John Sage was named a 2011 Purpose Prize Fellow by Civic Ventures' Encore Careers.
- Bridges To Life received the 2011 Social Innovator Award for the state of Texas.
- John Sage was awarded the Inaugural 2011 American Leadership Forum Public Service Award.
- John Sage was one of three finalists representing our Houston Astros for the 2009 People All Stars Among Us award.
- John Sage was selected as the first recipient of the Bert Thompson Pioneer Award for Community and Restorative Justice, given at the National Conference on Restorative Justice in May, 2009.
- In 2008, John Sage was recipient of the 2008 Liberty Bell Award and the 2008 Samaritan Spirit Award.
- Recipient of a Governor's Criminal Justice Volunteer Award every year, 2001– 2010.
- Winner of the 2007 Dallas Cowboys Community Quarterback Award.
- John Sage was selected as a recipient of the 2004 Social Entrepreneurship Award given by the Manhattan Institute in New York City.
- Articles: Guideposts, Texas Monthly, Houston Chronicle, Greater Houston Weekly, Dallas Morning News, Austin American-Statesman, San Antonio Express-News, Beaumont Enterprise, Amarillo Globe News, Change Magazine, Stirrings Magazine, Mosaic newspaper, Faith Works magazine, Restorative Justice News, Texas Mediator, Crime Victims Report, Psychology Today, Baton Rouge

Advocate, Houston Weekly, Daily Texan, Chautauquan Daily, Offender Substance Abuse Report and various other victim advocate, prison ministry, and restorative justice publications.

- Books: The Bridges To Life program and volunteers have been given significant recognition in three books published in 2004 including *Restoring Peace: Using Lessons From Prison to Mend Broken Relationships,* by Kirk Blackard, a Bridges To Life volunteer.

- TV News features: *Houston* – Channel 2(NBC), Channel 8 (PBS), Channel 11(CBS), Channel 13(ABC): *Tyler* – Channel 56 (NBC), Channel 7 (ABC); *Austin* – Channel 24 (ABC); *Beaumont* – Channel 4 (NBC), Channel 6 (CBS), Channel 12 (ABC); *San Antonio* – Channel 29 (FOX).

MISSION STATEMENT

To connect communities to prisons in an effort to reduce the recidivism rate (particularly that resulting from violent crimes), reduce the number of crime victims, and enhance public safety.

SPIRITUAL MISSION

To minister to prisoners and victims in an effort to show them the transforming power of God's love and forgiveness.

FOUNDED

Bridges To Life was founded in November 1998 in Houston Texas by John Sage. BTL is a faith-based nonprofit corporation exempt under section 501(c)(3) of the Internal Revenue Code.

ECONOMIC AND SOCIETAL IMPACT

Crime is one of our country's most pressing social problems. It destroys the personal well-being of victims and perpetrators alike and impairs the public safety and financial stability of the entire country. In fact, 1 in every 33 adults in the United States is incarcerated (Bureau of Justice Statistics, 2010), at a cost of $75 billion annually (Center for Economic Policy and Research, 2010). And Texas is first in the nation in terms of property crime and inmate population. Yet, the criminal justice system focuses on punishing and warehousing criminals with little or no emphasis on rehabilitation. Many released inmates return to prison. Our country is experiencing massive incarceration, and victims of crime are largely voiceless in the system.

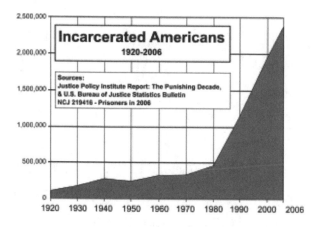

Victims. Each year thousands of Texans are the victims of crime at the hands of others. According to the U.S. Bureau of Justice (2004) Texas is ranked number seven (7) in the number of crimes per 100,000 people; and in 2007 nearly 492 out of every

100,000 people in Harris County were the victim of a violent crime (U.S. Department of Justice). Crime affects our sense of well being and safety, and it often adversely impacts families and children. Victims of violent crime often experience an adversarial justice system and few social supports (OVCTTC, 2008).

Children and families are also victimized by the criminal activity and incarceration of a loved one. According to a 2010 report by the Pew Charitable Trusts, approximately 1 in 28 children in the United States is impacted by the incarceration of a parent (2010). Families with loved ones imprisoned experience a higher incidence of poverty and homelessness. And, as a result of emotional issues such as shame and loss, one in ten children of incarcerated parents will be incarcerated later in life (Community Action Network 2009).

Offenders. The United States, home of 5 percent of the world's population, holds 25 percent of the world's prisoners. One out of every 140 U.S. residents is in jail or prison, and Texas holds approximately 154,000 prisoners each year—50 percent of whom are incarcerated for violent crimes. In fact, the rate of incarceration in Texas is 31 percent higher than the national average. Each year, some 70,000 of these offenders are released back into the Texas civilian population, and more than 15,000 are released into the Houston area (Texas Criminal Justice Coalition, 2009).

Juvenile Need. In Texas, approximately 140,000 youth are arrested annually, 80,000 of whom are referred to the probation system. Taxpayers and victims will incur an estimated $2 million dollars for each young person who becomes a career criminal (Texas Public Policy Foundation, February 2011). Research shows that incarceration is less effective than evidence-based juvenile probation programs. Every youth redirected from Texas Youth Commission (TYC) saves taxpayers about $80,000 a year. For all but the most serious and high-risk offenders, incarceration increases the likelihood of re-offending, as lower-risk youths are negatively influenced by higher-risk peers and positive bonds with their family, church and community are frayed (Texas Public Policy Foundation, May 2010).

Recidivism. An offender is considered to have recidivated if, after release from prison, he/she commits a new crime or violates the terms of his/her supervision within 3 years and is again incarcerated. In 2009, more than 725,000 people were released from state prisons. Half of these individuals are expected to be re-incarcerated within three years (Bureau of Justice Statistics 2011). Individuals that have been incarcerated face a multitude of challenges upon their release—including difficulty finding employment, a lack of family and social support and substance abuse issues—that often times lead to re-offending behaviors. As Bridges To Life grows, its positive effect is helping to change the attitude of the prison system regarding rehabilitation.

Appendix B

PARTICIPANT FEEDBACK

VICTIM VOLUNTEER COMMENTS

- Allowing us to tell our story gives us the opportunity to verbalize for others and ourselves the pain we have endured which is important in the long journey of healing and wholeness in life.
- Participating in the BTL program is beneficial for victims of crime because it releases pent up emotions and gets you out of self and into helping another person or people.
- Putting ourselves in each others shoes educates us both and brings out compassion and freedom of feelings on both sides!
- Provides the space, the time, the tools, and the opportunity for victims to focus on their own journey of healing.
- Participating in the Bridges To Life program has helped me to better understand and solidify my forgiveness journey.
- We know we may make an impact, by putting a face to the crime, on the lives of people who may otherwise go out and commit those same crimes again.
- Telling one's story is a vital part of the healing process. It has also allowed me to watch myself grow emotionally and spiritually, providing a ruler of sorts by which to gauge my growth.
- Telling one's story is essential to the healing process.
- When you go through horrific events in your life and you know that God pulled you through it with His Unconditional Love, it needs to be shared. If my speaking to prisoners can uplift and change one life, I am very satisfied.

- Bridges To Life has helped me by allowing me to share the positive lessons I have learned from my negative experiences with people who can benefit from the knowledge.
- Until the offender has to put a face to crime, they will never change their ways. You have to get to their heart first to change the mind.
- I have learned how to forgive, because I have come face to face with people who have committed similar crimes, and have seen that change of heart is possible.
- BTL has helped me understand a little better why people do bad things. But the best thing I receive as a victim volunteer is seeing that hearts can be changed.
- Participating in Bridges To Life helped me to get control and understanding back in my life.
- I never in my wildest dreams thought I would empathize with those behind bars. The common feelings shared by both the offenders and the victims are incredible.
- Hope...That's what this program is about. The healing is amazing on both sides.
- I am here to make a difference! I want to save the world one person at a time!
- Forgiveness affords the victim with great relief from a heavy burden.
- Bridges To Life gives hope to the victim volunteer that the inmates will not commit other crimes against other people. This is the great hope of all who participate in the Bridges To Life Program.
- I really think telling my story to prisoners helped empower me. I felt I was directly targeting the audience that needed to hear it the most.
- This program allows us to share, tell and demonstrate first hand to offenders the effect that crime has had on our lives.
- You never get over the tragic loss of a loved one, but you learn how to live your life differently without them, knowing that you are positively contributing to the lives of others.

OFFENDER COMMENTS

- The stories I heard made me think life is too short to be locked up.
- I got to see crime through both eyes and I don't wanna ever see that hurt again.
- I understand that everyone has troubles and deals with the same temptations I do. I also recognize that I actually put my victim through so much that I don't want no other person to go through that.
- I received compassion, strength, honesty, dignity, courage, faith. Mostly the faith in self to get out and make something good out of a bad.
- I learned to be responsible as an individual. Owning up to my actions, instead of denying them all the time.
- I don't want to hurt people the way I seen and heard about in this program.
- I've learned from victim's love and to love my neighbor as myself.
- I realize that it could be my family suffering because of a crime someone committed against me or even my family.
- It showed me that the victim is a person with a life and loved ones the same as I do. They also feel the pain of what has happened to them.
- I got a chance to learn about choices and know that with the right choices no one will ever be a victim of nothing I've done. I won't return.
- It's a good eye opener to those who only see one side of things.
- What I received the most about the program is that they taught me how to love and forgive again. They taught me how to speak what's on my mind.
- It does have an impact on your life. It makes you think and dig deep into your heart to search for answers.
- It helps us to look at the whole picture and to come face to face with the reality of what we did and who we affected.
- After hearing the victim's stories I never want to commit another crime and be the cause of someone's pain.

- The interest of free people giving of their time, people who have been victimized by people like me, put to rest a lot of my cynicism towards society.
- The program gave me a chance to look deep into myself and understand that all my actions have a ripple effect. I involve others in my life even if it is involuntary.
- It will give me important tools to use but only God and myself can truly be responsible for my life.
- I don't ever want to hurt anyone else, this program have given me lesson on treating peoples the way I want to be treated.
- I received love from those whom I did not expect love.
- I have changed my way of thinking. My whole life is in perspective.
- It's shown me victims up close, and shown me how not to rationalize, justify my actions. It's also shown me that my crimes weren't victimless as I always wanted to believe.
- This has reinforced my resolve and given me a mission to help others as I have been helped.
- The program helped me to feel self worth that I had lost.
- I received a lot of respect and discipline and learned to listen to the other person's story because we all have a story to tell and someone has to hear it.
- I learned that my problems are nothing compared to some of the others.
- My group gave me the feeling that they really cared.
- The program gives you a look from both sides. You get to see the pain and hurt you cause, so it helps you not to want to cause pain or hurt.
- This program has been the most productive and profound program that I've ever been involved in. I pray that God will open doors for me, that I can share the wisdom gained from this program.
- It gave me a better understanding of myself and that there is no such thing as a victimless crime.
- I understand now what I do to society and I don't want to hurt family or friends anymore.

NOTES

Biblical quotations are from the *Life Application Bible* unless otherwise noted. Original copies of material quoted from volunteers are in the Bridges To Life files.

Chapter 8: Confession
1   Jung as quoted in Joan Borysenko, *Guilt is the Teacher, Love is the Lesson* (New York: Warner Books, Inc., 1990), p. 179.

Chapter 9: Repentance
1   Richard Owen Roberts, *Repentance* (Wheaton, Illinois: Crossway Books, 2002), p. 178.
2   C. S. Lewis, *Mere Christianity*, p. 56.
3   Richard Owen Roberts, *Repentance*, p. 108.
4   Rachel Naomi Remen, *Kitchen Table Wisdom* (New York: Riverhead Books, 1996), p. 219.

Chapter 10: Forgiveness
1   Fred Luskin, *Forgive for Good: A Proven Prescription for Health and Happiness* (New York: HarperCollins Publishers, Inc., 2002), p. 68.
2   Samuel R. Todd, Jr., *An Introduction to Christianity*, p. 109.
3   C. S. Lewis, *Mere Christianity*, p. 115.

Chapter 11: Reconciliation
1   Laura Davis, *I Thought We'd Never Speak Again* (New York: HarperCollins Publishers, Inc. 2002), p. 27.

Chapter 12: Restitution

1   C. S. Lewis, *The Screwtape Letters* (New York: HarperCollins Publishers, Inc. 1942), p. 66.

BOOK ORDER FORM

RESTORING PEACE

Using Lessons From Prison to Mend Broken Relationships

BRIDGES TO LIFE PROGRAM EDITION

Book Price: $10 X _____ books $ _____

Shipping & Handling:
     $3 (1st book) plus $1 each additional book $ _____

                                   Total $ _____

☐   Check/Money Order   Payable to "Bridges To Life"

☐   Master Card/Visa   _____
                                               Credit Card Number

_____   _____
          Signature   Expiration Date

Name _____ Street _____

City/State _____ Zip _____ Telephone _____

Bridges To Life
P.O. Box 570895
Houston, Texas 77257-0895

Restoring Peace may also be ordered by credit card at www.bridgestolife.org.